Gavin Calver is the younger son of Dr Clive and Mrs
Ruth Calver. Clive was for many years General
Director of Evangelical Alliance UK, and is now
President of World Relief, a Christian relief and
development organisation based in Baltimore, USA.

Youth for Christ (YFC)

Having been started by the American evangelist Billy Graham in 1946, over 50 years later Youth for Christ still exists for the purpose of taking the good news relevantly to every young person in Britain. As one of the most dynamic Christian organisations, its members go out on the streets, into schools and communities, and pioneer new and meaningful methods of reaching young people where they are at.

The staff, trainees and volunteers currently reach over 58,000 young people weekly. God has used YFC to impact the lives of millions throughout Britain. There are over 50 local centres, from the Isle of Wight to Inverness, as well as hundreds of churches linked to the movement. Among many other things, YFC invests in future evangelists and youth workers, provides outreach and discipleship resources for church-based youth work, offers residential opportunities, and places a growing emphasis on peer-to-peer evangelism. British Youth for Christ is part of a wider international family operating in over 120 nations worldwide.

For more information about anything to do with Youth for Christ in Britain, for prayer points or latest news please visit www.yfc.co.uk or telephone 0121-550-8055.

Disappointed with JESUS?

Why do so many young people give up on God?

Gavin Calver

MONARCH
BOOKS

Oxford, UK, and Grand Rapids, Michigan

First published by Monarch Books
(a publishing imprint of Lion Hudson plc) in the UK 2004,
Mayfield House, 256 Banbury Road, Oxford OX2 7DH.
Tel: +44 (0) 1865 302750 Fax: +44 (0) 1865 302757
Email: monarch@lionhudson.com
www.lionhudson.com

ISBN 1 85424 649 6

Distributed by:
Marston Book Services Ltd, PO Box 269, Abingdon, Oxon OX14 4YN.

British Library Cataloguing Data
A catalogue record for this book is available
from the British Library.

Printed in England.

Acknowledgements

I'd really like to thank Monarch Books, and Tony Collins in particular, for sharing my vision. Their encouragement in and commitment to the production of this book have been invaluable. I would also like to thank my wife Anne, my mum and dad, and the rest of my family, for their unwavering support and love throughout this challenging project, and life in general. Thanks to some very close friends as well who have shared this journey with me: Danny, Jessy, Ben, Phil and Abigail in particular.

I'd like to thank the churches that have played a key part in my life. Thank you very much Ichthus, Forest Hill, Stanmore Baptist Church, and most recently Fatherless Barn Evangelical Church. I'm very grateful to Youth for Christ for providing me with an opportunity to try and make a difference among the young of Britain. Long may we continue to share the Good News of Jesus with them. Finally, and most importantly, I'd like to thank the Lord who has changed me inside out, upside down and back to front ever since I fully surrendered my life to Him.

Dedication

To the church.
May we grow to be the
Bride of Christ more and more,
and change our world for Him.

Contents

Foreword

*O*ne of the great joys of growing older is
that you get to see what happens when God gets hold
of young lives and begins to shape them.

I recently sat spellbound as Gavin Calver lectured
over 100 preachers, many of them twice his age, on
the techniques of evangelistic preaching.

It was hard to believe that this was the chap I'd
known when he was a spotty teenager and an ardent
Wimbledon fan. It was clear that God had been at
work!

This book gives us an insight into the struggles of
those intervening years. Struggles with the church,
struggles with the faith, and struggles with surviving
the pain of adolescence.

I hope it will help a lot of young people who are
still travelling that rollercoaster ride. If you feel that
no one quite understands what you're going through,
I think you'll find Gavin's story refreshingly honest
and supportive.

A lot of parents, youth workers and pastors would
do well to read this book, too. We also need to listen
to what Gavin is saying. I'm only too aware that my
own experience of adolescence is but a dim memory,

and that much of my impatience with my own teenage sons a few years ago stemmed from a basic lack of understanding of what they were feeling. I wish I'd had an opportunity to read this book long before it was written when I was really "going through it" as a parent!

Don't let the title put you off! This is a book with a happy ending. If you think that adolescence is a total disaster for everyone... hang on in there! God is often doing something very special... in spite of our best efforts. Gavin is living proof that there really is life beyond adolescence.

Revd. Dr Rob Frost,
Director of Share Jesus International

Preface

Some years ago I witnessed a piece of drama I have never been able to get out of my mind. It was in the Big Top at Spring Harvest, and part of the tent was filled with young people. Somebody began to read out the statistics of the rate at which those young people were leaving the church. As he did so, groups of young people stood up and left the tent. At age twelve and thirteen there were just a few, but moving through the later teenage years it became a tide as hundreds thronged the aisles to walk out of church life – some of them forever.

Many of us have known the sheer frustration of seeing thriving youth ministries suddenly decimated when the young people hit their late teens. This book helps to explain why this happens and, even more importantly, tells us how to turn the tide. I was captivated as I read it, both as a parent and as somebody who is passionate about prodigals. It takes the lid off what makes it easy in church life for some to leave and so very hard for them to return.

I have never read a book on this topic written by somebody so young, and therefore so near to what teenagers and those in their early twenties actually experience in church. I believe *Disappointed with Jesus* is a "must read" for all who care about young people. Gavin Calver warns us, scares us and encourages us – sometimes all on the same page! I thank God he has written *Disappointed with Jesus*. It is a book for our time.

Rob Parsons,
Executive Director, Care for the Family,
January 2004

Introduction

I was at a conference when a colleague of mine brought someone to speak to me. This particular someone was a young lady who had been struggling with everything she was facing. She had grown up in a Christian home, with parents who were involved in public ministry. Her dad was well respected in the local community as a church pastor and everyone in the village knew exactly who her parents were, and, by association, who she was. She was always known as someone's child, as opposed to an individual in her own right. The other difficulty was that someone would always be more than happy to mention to her parents any wrong thing that she was seen doing. Locally she was anything other than anonymous. It all grew too much for her.

As a result, she found it very difficult to have any sort of faith for herself. She'd been in such a Christian goldfish bowl throughout her formative years that she'd never really needed to think about being a Christian for herself. Everyone else had lived it for her, and now that she had left home she simply couldn't stand on her own two spiritual feet. She had been hurt; she felt inadequate; and as a consequence of what had gone on around her she was browned off with church – though she claimed to be disappointed with Jesus.

I found this story devastating, as it highlighted many of the difficulties young people face when they grow up in a Christian home. They are expected to behave extra well. The faith they feel they should defend may be their parents', not their own. The problems are just accentuated if the parents are pivotal figures in the local (or in my case national) Christian landscape. This young woman's story showed me quite how fine is the line between young people developing their own faith, and rejecting it. She told me her brother had embraced the faith with open arms, having grown up under exactly the same conditions.

This whole incident triggered off a number of thoughts in my mind. Why do Christian young people struggle so much with growing up into faith? How come this girl was finding it all too hard? Why do we create such a pressure cooker for our young people that the drop-out rate becomes so high? How come other faith groups seem to hold on to their people more effectively? Why do so many leave the church? Where have all my peers gone? What are the reasons for the situation? Please can I have some answers, Lord? I was incredibly confused and wanted some clarity in my own mind.

As a young person, I myself attended what seemed at the time to be a flourishing church youth group. It was affiliated to a very charismatic church and seemed to be cutting-edge, in Christians terms at least. If one youth group in the area was going to produce many young Christians, then it was the one I attended. They had their own youth-orientated building, played the right songs, and incorporated decks into the worship well before most churches had even heard of them.

This was a specific youth church, and if young people couldn't find faith and fulfilment in Christ *here*, then where could they find it? Yet the test of time has proved that the many youth-orientated elements there were not sufficient to stem the tide. Of the ten to fifteen friends with whom I shared the experience of growing up in a Christian context, only one is really going on with the Lord today. What a truly appalling statistic! I've always wanted to do something to prevent the same fate befalling others, yet have never quite known how I could help.

Back at the conference I began chatting to those I was with. I was going to have to make some sort of response. It was one conversation too many, coming as it did on the back of so many similar discussions. I had finally had enough of young people from Christian homes leaving the church, and knew that the Lord wanted me to respond.

The next day, during the final meeting, I felt the Lord speaking very clearly to me. I was stunned by what I heard. I should write a book about some of my personal struggles and those of the individuals around me. No way, I thought. I had finished a Bible college degree some 18 months earlier and had decided halfway through my dissertation never again to write anything longer than a postcard.

Yet the wrestling didn't last too long. Much as I felt

a lack of ecstasy at the prospect, I knew I had to try. I couldn't sit back and hear more stories of doom and gloom while knowing that I could make a difference.

I'm not claiming to have all – or even nearly all – of the answers. I just have a deep sense that explaining things from my point of view may be helpful. Parents often complain that their children are not speaking to them, so I'm trying to offer the parent a way in to the mind of the adolescent. Obviously the issues will be different for other young people, yet I believe that an awful lot of the principles will be the same. I hope to break down some of the walls. I also hope to show people that they are not facing these struggles alone. It can often feel as if no one understands, so I want to show that others have been there too.

The specific aim of this book is to help more adolescents make it in their faith. I long for a generation to rise up, in the steps of so many great Christians who were converted as teenagers, and really shape this world for an eternity. Many Christian heroes were converted as teenagers, such as Charles Spurgeon (aged 15), George Whitefield (16), William Booth (15), C T Studd (16), James Hudson Taylor (15), D L Moody (18), Amy Carmichael (15) and Billy Graham (17), and then changed their surroundings for Jesus. It *can* happen again!

Many of today's adolescents could turn out to be such world-changers. According to the Christian Research Association, 75% of Christians were converted before the age of 20.[1] This means that we have to act fast and reach as many young people as possible. If we can reach these young people, then they in turn can reach their peers. We must make far greater efforts with those of this age.

If we can keep adolescents interested and active in their faith and in the church throughout their teenage years, then the chances are that they will remain for a lifetime – with 70 years of Christian service ahead of them. However, if they leave they may not come back to church until they're middle-aged, if ever. I long for these young folk to remain in church and become effective Christians.

So please join me on a journey through adolescence. Let's keep our young people in church; let's turn around all the negative statistics quoted at us, and let's see this planet changed for the sake of the King!

Gavin Calver
Halesowen
January 2004

1   Son Of A Preacher Man

*I*t all began in November 1979 on a bathroom floor in Wolverhampton. Gavin Jonathan Eric
Calver faced the world and its turbulent reality for
the very first time.

The birth of a child is a very exciting moment in
the lives of any parents. Yet for the Christian couple
there is a massive added element. Here into the world
comes not just a new life, but also a gift from God,
formed in the womb by the hands of the King. In the
Christian context, the dreams for this child
inevitably take on new and fresh meanings. Hopes for
the next Martin Luther, John Wesley, Billy Graham –
or maybe even a Clive Calver? If not, then at least for
a full-hearted servant of the Lord.

It is so easy to empathise. If you have discovered
eternal truth, then the most natural instinct is to see
your offspring follow the same truth. This is the
source of pressures and conflicts that can polarise
parent and child during the later years of adolescence. For the child of parents in public Christian
ministry, the pressures can be intensified and can
make the whole voyage of discovery even more taxing, as this son of a preacher man can testify!

However, we needn't deal with teenage angst just yet. This new life brings renewed hope, joy and possibility. No longer is it just about the couple themselves; now there is another life, utterly dependent upon them. The spiritual input into a child's life in these early days is as important as anything else. Even though other things may seem more immediately necessary in order to help the child to grow up fit and healthy, early spiritual input into the child's life is essential to its development.

I remember many of my early days with great fondness. Despite being so heavily accident-prone that my body was regularly adorned with plaster of Paris, these early years were a wonderful time. I particularly enjoyed prayers before bed and on special occasions my mum would sing to me as I went to sleep. I would also love it when she would go downstairs and sing worship songs whilst playing the piano. If I listened really carefully, I could hear her through the floor. It gave me such a sense of peace. I loved the fact that she sang Christian songs; after all, what else would she be singing at the piano?

The whole "God thing" went unquestioned. It all just made good sound sense and was a mandatory part of living. If there was a God in the sky who loved us all, sought to be our friend, and wanted to look after us, then this seemed like a wonderful thing. Considering how little we were putting in we seemed to be getting a good deal from this God! My parents believed all that stuff, so there was no way it could be wrong, was there?

How could such a young child even begin to comprehend the wonder and majesty that is the King of kings? Such complexities are far too great even for the sharpest and most developed of minds. There's nothing wrong with a child's limited view and understanding of God. In many ways it is the mind of the child that the adult Christian is taught to attempt to replicate. Jesus Himself said, "I tell you the truth, unless you change and become like little children, you will never enter the kingdom of heaven. Therefore, whoever humbles himself like this child is the greatest in the kingdom of heaven" (Matthew 18:3–4). We could all do with being a bit more like children.

For young children themselves the church is a safe environment in which to learn many of life's early lessons. Within the framework of church children's work they can begin to develop both in thought and behaviour. Historically, Sunday school has been educational. The church would take care of the schooling of many and was a societal (as well as a spiritual) necessity in a time when education was not freely available to all. Even today an element of this church-based education still remains. Perhaps the need for formal education has died out in Sunday schools, but lessons for life (such as social skills) can be learnt here very effectively in a safe environment, as opposed to more vicious environments such as the school playground. Other places will teach these lessons if the church won't.

Young children are in by far the best age group for inviting their peers to church. There is no sense of embarrassment in inviting one's unchurched friends to a church group. From playing football to listening to Bible stories, the primary-school age group is seemingly the one era when both Christians and non-Christians can meet. There is little hierarchy amongst the children at this stage and it is remarkable that all comers can feel at home in such a Christian setting.

The early years seem to be one of the few times when I have heard a number of people referring to church as "fun". This element of enjoyment plays a huge part. Why shouldn't church be fun? Surely a Jesus who desires His people to be joyful would hope that His church would be described as "fun", at least from time to time. What do we do as we grow up that makes church so boring and irrelevant to those who aren't part of the Christian community? Why must we be so *sensible*? We lose people this way!

Many churches seem to set about things the wrong way. Congregations drone out protracted hymns on a Sunday morning about how happy they are to have a friend like Jesus, and yet they look as if they are starring in a funeral. They talk about sharing their faith with their community with love, and yet they look as though, if they smiled too quickly, their faces would crack in two. Is this really "contagious Christianity"?

A good friend whom I work with at Youth for Christ told me about one of his mates. His friend was from a Christian home, but along with many others had become increasingly disillusioned with the church. It simply wasn't "scratching where it itched", and so this guy left. He was incessantly nagged from home about going to church, as his parents feared for the child that they thought they were losing. This pressure from home only exacerbated an already strained situation. As the parental pressure hit home, so the chasm between young person and church grew.

This guy threw down a challenge to my friend. Thinking he was onto a winner, he said, "If you find me a church that's not boring, I'll go." My friend took up this challenge and invited this guy to his church. The church was an emerging cell-model type and at the end of the evening the guy openly declared that this had been the first time that he'd attended a church of any description and not found himself utterly bored. He was genuinely surprised that boredom wasn't a compulsory part of church attendance. By the end of the service he was still wide awake!

The following Sunday the guy took no persuading; he was desperate to go again. When the two of them had arrived for the second week in a row, everyone in the group was asked to say what the highlight of the previous week had been. To everyone's surprise he piped up first, and said that for him the highlight had been going to church the week before. This guy was simply stunned that church needn't be completely dull.

Why should church be boring? My Jesus is totally exciting and worth jumping for joy about. So why can't we represent this in church? We need to encourage our children to keep their childlike enthusiasm, fun and laughter as they grow in the church environment. If they keep their fun then perhaps some of this joy might rub off onto some of us older ones who've forgotten that faith and boredom are extremes.

I was reading a book recently about how we can reach and keep young people in the church. In one of the focus groups it was suggested that, in order to make church more appealing to young people, we should "add some laughs" or "have a happy week".[2] How alarming that this is how we're perceived. What have we done so wrong that we are now seen as a group of people who *need* to have some fun or even a happy week? The biggest lesson that every one of us can take from the early life of a child is to enjoy life and to be able to see church as fun and as a place of vibrant, contagious community. It would have an immense effect on our mission to the world as well as on the spiritual health of those already within the Christian community.

It is very easy to look at the early years of a young person's life and think that he or she has a lot to learn. In reality we can learn an awful lot from *them*. We need to encourage them and in turn be encouraged. We need to help and teach them, whilst being taught ourselves. We need to make them part of the church community and a vital reflection of what it means to be a local expression of God's love. But we must move on. The young baby is rapidly growing, and is now in fact an eight-year-old halfway through junior school. Not yet a sweaty, hairy adolescent, but a child with a mind of his or her own.

2   Are My Parents Right?

*E*very primary-school class has its own bully. Mine was no different. That colossus controlled the playground by fear and intimidation, and employed his worshippers as his personal foot soldiers. He had gone through quite a growth spurt, and towered above his schoolfriends. He had a very aggressive manner and would gain authority over everyone else through sheer brute force. In the playground football arena he won every game that ever took place through a personal interpretation of each rule.

In smaller schools, one or perhaps two bullies will govern the primary-school environment. In a school population often totalling fewer than 200 people, split into year groups of fewer than 30, it can be easy for an individual to take control. My class bully was a guy called Peter. He was a giant. I was no midget, but he was huge. You could fit both of my legs into one of his. He was the only guy who really had muscles, which he was very happy to show to any of the girls. If Peter was your friend then you could be a very powerful person, but if he was your enemy then you would be in no end of trouble.

For the first few years of primary school I accepted Peter's way of being without any question. He was in charge; no one else seemed to have a problem with this, so why should I? Peter had nothing much against me. This made me pretty safe at school and as such I was happy for him to get on with things; the unspoken arrangement was fine. After all, we all need leadership, don't we? I knew nothing different from his way of leading and so accepted it quite easily. Not to mention that you'd have had to be either very brave or particularly stupid to question Peter, the man-mountain.

One particular term, the way that I saw things began to change.

Up until this point I'd had a very simple outlook on life. Then, aged nine, I started to see things differently. Why *should* Peter be nasty to people? What right did he have to act like this? Why did no one ever tell him to get lost? Who did he think he was? All these thoughts came to a head when Peter picked on my good friend Richard one Friday afternoon. Richard thought his team had beaten Peter's in the lunchtime football match. Peter had miscounted the goals, argued Richard. But Peter's team never lost. We'd all been at school together for over four years; we played every lunchtime, and no one had ever known Peter's team to lose. Yet Richard was sticking to his argument and professing victory for the team he had been playing on.

Peter was not prepared to let this lie. He cornered Richard and started pushing him about. Richard was to be made an example. No one would ever dare question Peter's authority again. The immediate implications for Richard were intensified by the fact that he was your archetypal primary-school weed, the antithesis of Peter. Where Peter had biceps, Richard had matchstick arms; where Peter had eyes that could cut you in two, Richard had thick-rimmed NHS spectacles; where Peter had a ready-made insult for every occasion, Richard was quiet and well spoken. The contrasts were endless. Richard was a lamb ready for the slaughter, and slaughtering defenceless classmates was a skill that Peter had mastered over the years.

I was on the other side of the playground when the commotion drew my attention. From across a crowded playground I could make out the figures of Peter and Richard and had no doubts at all about what was going on. Along with many others I'd had enough of Peter's antics. If he was picking a fight with Richard then he was picking one with me, too. Filled with a surge of adrenalin I rushed over. In stark contrast to Richard, who looked utterly terrified, Peter was as animated, vociferous and aggressive as ever.

I elbowed my way through to where Richard was standing and told him to run away. Suddenly the reality of what I was doing struck me for the first time. In his fighting pose Peter looked bigger than ever. He was huge, and had his fists ready for action. But I couldn't back down now. My deep-felt anxiety was matched with adrenalin and for some inexplicable reason I did what had previously been unthinkable; I punched Peter in the face. He seemed genuinely stunned that anyone could have the audacity to do such a thing. A combination of shock, anger and (I'd like to think) even a little pain flitted across the face of this nine-year-old dictator. I too was now utterly terrified!

I had to take a couple of fierce blows to the head before my princess came to the rescue. Not until that day (and at no point afterwards) had I ever viewed our middle-aged dinner lady in quite that light. She became my heroine as she strode gracefully across the playground towards where we were and started roaring at us. On any other day her bellowing was horrible, but on this day she sounded as sweet as a bird singing in a tree. She was about to save me from a level of pain and public humiliation that my nine-year-old frame would not have been able to handle. For that moment she was a princess, my equivalent to a knight in shining armour.

She grabbed both Peter and me by the arm and took us to the edge of the playground. Here we were made to stand either side of her in silence against the fence. For once, enduring this punishment felt like heaven. I knew that I'd been either very brave or very stupid in taking Peter on. Why did I do such a thing? Would I ever recover from the inevitable rematch in the park after school? I couldn't back down now, could I?

As the day reached its end I was fearfully anticipating a well-deserved mauling. I was dreading the walk of death from the classroom to the scene of the beating. To my great surprise, Peter didn't want to tear me into little pieces. He didn't desire to show any aggression towards me; in fact he wanted to be friends. He felt that we were better off together than we would ever be apart. My courage, such as it was, in taking him on had made me a bit too much of an effort for him to be bothered with! The key to becoming Peter's friend was to threaten his authority and force him to make you an ally instead. I never shared my discovery with anyone else; they would have to find it out for themselves.

That Friday lunchtime is important because it reminds me of the period in my life when I first started seeing things in a different way. Everything had previously been so simple and straightforward. But at the age of nine my whole world was being turned upside down. Not every child at school had a mummy and a daddy; some of my friends didn't think there was a God, and why should Peter control the playground? Suddenly the whole of life was open to debate.

As a younger child, it's all so simple. Everything you can see around you is all that there is. You think in a concrete way. For example, were you to show a five-year-old child a picture of a house and ask him what it was, he would say that the picture was his house. If you showed him a picture of a lady, then he'd say it was Mummy. As this child grows up, such pictures instead become *a* house or *a* lady. This is what is known as a change in understanding between concrete and abstract thinking. Though this change is not totally completed by the end of primary school, it certainly begins during a child's time at junior school. This is the exact process I was going through.

Life becomes increasingly confusing as the years roll on. The Christian child needs to be given the room to develop within the home and the church, and still deeply desires the backbone of truth that underpins the Christian faith. Yet all the previous certainties that the child could live by are now challenged. "Because Mummy says so" is no longer good enough. This all leads to a general feeling that the whole world has been turned upside down.

Children can become quite confused as their mental capacity grows and they are taught new things in school. Our pluralistic society means that, for example, they are taught about all faiths. What is right, which path leads to God, and what is truth anyway? Our kids are being taught that if it works for you then that's great. One of my favourite bands as a teenager was the Manic Street Preachers. They produced an album called *This is my truth, tell me yours!* This album title aptly sums up the situation.

Our young children are being taught that all truth is relative. How can a juvenile mind even hope to grapple with this post-modern, fluffy rubbish? Do we really think it's reasonable to ask a child to go from thinking concretely to relativism in just a few years? It is essential that we teach our Christian young that there *is* such a thing as absolute truth. In spite of what society may claim, we must let the future leaders of our church know that not *any* path to God is acceptable. Jesus is *the* Way, *the* Truth and *the* Life.

In the church setting, the older end of the primary-school age group is an interesting time. These kids need to be handled differently and they suddenly desire an alternative approach. We need to encourage them to express their new ways of thinking and to show their individuality. Some of these kids may be bullied at school for being different, but in the church setting we need to affirm individual differences, as these are what make us unique.

Many young people are bullied by playground dictators. The British NSPCC (National Society for the Prevention of Cruelty to Children) says that one in eight young adults has been bullied or discriminated against regularly in their childhood, and 10% of bullied children felt that bullying had long-term effects.[3] Churches must be a haven for the many young people who are struggling in the world outside. If they are welcomed in the church and not judged on superficial appearances, then they will feel affirmed and grow in confidence.

Children at this age will want to question things – something that the church and parents need to embrace. How we handle such questions will set the tone for many years to come. This will almost certainly be the first time they question different facets of the Christian faith. It definitely won't be the last.

From some children, Christianity will come under closer scrutiny than from others. It is helpful to let them ask. We need to have some knowledge of other faiths as well as of our own. With such an understanding it is easier to highlight the uniqueness of Christ. An obvious contrast with Islam, for example, can show straight away that, whilst our God is all about love, the god of Islam, Allah, is given 99 names, not one of which means love. The uniqueness of Christ is untouchable! This uniqueness must be made clear to young people so that they in turn can tell others.

Early education is over and what lies ahead is a steady progression towards adolescence. The challenges of the next ten years are going to be many times more taxing for adolescent, parents and church. These struggles will lead, by the grace of God, to the formation of people who will drive the church in years to come.

But how many will be lost along the way?

3   A Clash Of Views

*T*he transition from primary to secondary education is huge. Moving schools is the biggest ever change in a young person's life. Why doesn't the church prepare them for this? We really should. Parents don't really have a clue at this stage, but youth workers do. Through understanding youth culture and having a presence in local schools, youth workers are in touch with young people and can relate to the challenges involved in this great transition. They must connect with young people and help them through this change. If the church isn't helping young people at *this* time, then what hope is there?

The child who has finally found an identity, some level of acceptance and a place to belong (within the primary-school environment) must now venture out into the daunting new world of the secondary school. It is an enforced stepping out of one's comfort zone to enter into what can seem at the time like a den of lions.

A number of new problems for young people are created. They have to decide who they want to be. Many of the ways in which they behave in the early weeks of secondary school will set patterns that they will be unable to free themselves from for the rest of their schooldays. I can think of two or three people in my year at secondary school who behaved like cretins at the start and never quite shook off this reputation for the next seven years' worth of education. A few early misjudgements in behaviour can leave an individual typecast for the foreseeable future. I myself was typecast, and found it very hard.

Everyone seeks to be accepted and many feel that they need to be extraordinary to fit in. You are desperate for people to like you, so will go to any lengths in order to achieve this. Many people at my school would lie in order to be accepted. Their lives were not very exciting, so they glamorised them in order to seem more interesting. One guy had a dad who was supposedly a *ninja* – until parents' evening, when a small, gentle-looking man came in. His response of, "What's a ninja?" kind of gave the game away.

In contrast to a number of my peers, I lied not to be exciting but just to be normal. While others longed to have a more exotic background, I earnestly coveted the mundane. I wanted no one to discover what my dad did. It was getting harder to hide it too. He was in the media more now, and so people kept recognising the guy. I just wanted a dad who was a teacher or a doctor, as opposed to the leader of an evangelical organisation. I wanted to merge into the shadows instead of being seen as a child from a Bible-bashing background. Others lied in order to discover excitement; I lied to achieve normality.

A similar problem faces contestants in TV reality shows. Take *Big Brother*, for example. On this programme, if you behave stupidly at the start, then you can easily be seen as being like that in essence. Soon enough such a character will be voted off the show. Contestants have to learn how to behave in completely new surroundings, away from the safety of familiarity and long-term relationships – just as at a new school.

The problem for the child entering the secondary school is that as a rule he or she cannot leave so easily to start again elsewhere. Instead of a few weeks of torment, the adolescent must face up to seven years of playground strife. There aren't many groups of people that are regularly harsher than school kids (particularly in places such as inner London, where I went to school). The level of personal insult is exceptionally high, and the things that young people say to one another would seem incredibly offensive to anyone else. For some adolescents the whole thing is one long struggle.

The move to secondary school may require a complete change of public persona. At primary school, one lad had been perceived as one of the cool crowd. Life was fun and free. When this lad went to secondary school it was a different situation altogether. Among a far bigger crowd of people he was no longer so good at football, and neither was he seen as cool. Over the course of one summer he had changed from being someone people appreciated, respected and wanted to be like, to someone people didn't think anything of, had no time for and weren't prepared to build a relationship with. The poor lad was left not knowing what to do with his time.

This process was near-on soul-destroying. He'd spent the whole of his formative primary-school years as someone popular, but now, all of a sudden, his whole identity had been shifted. He did his best to reverse the trend, but he couldn't be the person that he used to be, because his social climate wouldn't allow it. Unfortunately, he became more and more of a recluse as the years wore on.

It is important that we should be aware of all of the issues of self-esteem that are involved in this mega-transition. As a church we need to support our young people through it. Just being there as a listening ear can be enough. This helps a young person to realise that, even if people at school don't care who she is, *God* does. Even if she's not accepted in the playground, there's another context outside, called the church, that will accept her wholeheartedly.

The young people are now in a situation in which they are desperate to prove themselves. This aspiration manifests itself in the home as well as the playground. The adolescent becomes increasingly confused and this can cause deep-rooted problems in the home. Between the ages of eleven and thirteen is when the real conflict often arises between a child and the culture of faith that he or she has been brought up in. Parents need to learn patience and awareness of this struggle. They must never take it all personally; it won't last forever.

The difficulties of moving to secondary school cannot on their own account for all such problems. The young person's body is starting to behave in unusual ways as he or she rapidly heads towards/into puberty. It is enough to make one shudder at quite how difficult this period in the young person's life is!

This is often the first time in their lives they are seeking a level of real independence from the family unit. They go to school, where they have to battle to be accepted – yet go home and try to fight for quite the opposite. It's so ironic that on one level the young people are desperately seeking to make it, be accepted and become part of the group, yet on the other hand they are doing everything they can to become independent of the family unit in which they *are* completely accepted. This doesn't mean that they genuinely don't want to be a part of the family, but the mixed messages all lead to great confusion.

A lot of the divisions in the previously harmonious family unit develop from the fact that the young adolescent has suddenly started thinking he or she is actually an adult. The child can start competing with one or both of the parents for roles within the family unit. The whole thing can become quite dysfunctional.

The independence issue is interesting. It is something that young people crave only when it suits their agenda. A number of young girls seek to have a clothes allowance from their parents. This seems like a wonderful idea. They'll be able to get loads of clothes and will be so much happier once they can choose exactly when and where to buy them. However, it takes them no time at all to realise that they're getting less *with* the allowance than they were before. The desire for independence is an attempt to grow up too soon.

It's always interesting to see what happens when it all goes wrong. The British comic Harry Enfield came up with the hilarious character, the teenager Kevin. I'm sure many of you know exactly who I mean. Basically he's a teenage boy who has no respect for his parents. He wears his clothes really baggy; his hair is a mess and he is convinced he is mature enough to be independent. His regular response to anything he disagrees with is, "That's *so* unfair!"

When Kevin is asked to clear up his mess, his customary retort is, "I'm not your slave." He takes every given opportunity to inform his parents, with as much compassion as his years allow, that he hates them. However, in the feature film based on the adventures of Kevin and his best friend and sidekick Perry, *Kevin and Perry Go Large*, it is interesting to see what Kevin does when things get tough. He and Perry have a major fall-out and, when it seems that everything is too much for Kevin to cope with, what does he do? He turns to his parents for help and support and is delightful to them – in fact he needs them and their love. Soon enough he and Perry sort out their differences, and at this point he rejects his parents once more.

For parents it is important always to be there at the ready. This is incredibly hard, but it is essential nonetheless. The child who claims independence and may even claim to hate you still needs you desperately! Parental authority may be questioned, but at this age a child still craves the structure and security of the family unit. With all the pressures they are facing in the big wide world, somewhere to call "home" is essential. Ideally, having a church to call "home" as well can make all the difference. In the church environment the parent and the adolescent both get supported.

Adolescents may have convinced themselves that they are older and more mature and experienced than they actually are. I don't think I ever told my parents that one of my friends and I ran away from home one afternoon when we were eleven. Come teatime we were hungry, and decided that, with our rebellion complete, it was time to go home for dinner. We wanted to be independent when it suited us, but the minute we needed something we were happy to be dependent once more.

It is important for parents to be united at this point. They need to work at it together and not respond to their children's attempts to rile them. One Christian parent said, "Parents need to know what pushes their child's emotional buttons (e.g. washing up, mealtime discussion, etc.) and not allow these to engulf the situation. Only pick the battles that are worth it." The parent can make the situation ten times worse than it need to be, or alternatively a great deal easier for the young person. This all plays a huge part in the process of adolescence.

The church too must be there to help. Understanding and supporting the change of schools needs to become second nature to church children's and youth work. If the young people can feel supported throughout then we can help to minimise the effects of this most dramatic change. The church must be on hand to help.

We end this chapter with the picture of a twelve-year-old adolescent knocking on the door labelled "Teenager". There are many more degrees of difficulty to face in the imminent future. This is all very difficult for the onlooking parents and church, but it is also no walk in the park for the adolescents themselves. During this period God may feel a million miles away from it all for both the parents and the young person. However, we must hang in there, because if the church can keep them through the struggles until the later teenage years, then we have them for life.

4   I Hate Church!

I was never an angel in church youth groups, and I had a partner in crime called Danny. We became best mates when we were twelve and thirteen, and from that moment onwards we were largely inseparable.

Danny and I were utter pains. We would do our best to disrupt anything for an easy laugh and were a youth leader's nightmare. Never really malicious or aggressive, we were certainly cheeky.

Danny and I would always turn up to everything together. We were synonymous with one another. We regularly led one another astray. If possible we'd try and lead others astray too. Why cause mischief on your own when it was so easy to influence others? Every youth group has a Danny and Gavin, but very few know quite how to handle them.

On one particular Sunday morning, Danny and I set off for youth group together. As we turned the corner into the grounds of one of the church's buildings we saw our youth group sitting in a circle outside.

To our astonishment, on arrival we were greeted with great hostility. Granted, we were a little late, but the situation wasn't that bad. We were told in no uncertain terms to go back to where we'd come from, as we weren't welcome there. We were now officially banned from attending at all for six months. There was some garbled justification to do with thinking about our actions, but by this point we'd closed our ears to anything that our Sunday school teacher had to say. What an interesting method of trying to keep young people in the church. We were being forced out!

I was far more incensed by all of this than Danny was. I was really annoyed by the fact that we had been turned away. I clearly remember turning to Danny and saying, with as much meaning and authority as I could muster, "I hate church!" I simply couldn't believe that we'd been rejected. I knew the Bible quite well and couldn't understand how a group that allegedly followed the example of the Son of God, who "hung out" with tax collectors, lepers and prostitutes, could be so violently against two young minor rogues. Yes, we could be trouble, but in this instance we'd done nothing worse than turn up a few minutes later than the rest.

When the rest of my family returned from church, Danny went home. Soon enough it was time for Sunday lunch. Mum had a conversation with a couple of my siblings about their time at church that morning, and then inevitably it was my turn. I had a now well-practised retort: "I hate church!" I began to explain why, and you could immediately see the combination of hurt and concern on my mum's face.

I knew how to play my mum. To get back at my youth leader I was now straight down the line. Forget church, I hated it. I could have an effect on Mum that my sisters couldn't. No one had taught me how to play my mum; it was in my nature. Boys don't do it to dads; it's mums they can play. One would say things to get at Mum because she loves Jesus. Mums don't despair. Most of it isn't meant: it's just a hard time of discovery for young people. I talk about it now because the best thing that a parent can do is to try to understand where a young person is coming from, his strategy and his tactics. If this can happen, the situation becomes more understandable and bearable.

What should my youth leader have done? She should have cornered both Danny and me, individually. I should have been pulled aside, because if you split the partnership you divide and conquer. A significant adult, such as a youth worker, should get in amongst the peers. I longed for a relationship with my youth worker which was separate from Danny. She didn't seem to want this, so for security Danny and I joined together. If we'd had a decent relationship with our youth leader we would have been far more reluctant to breeze in late. Without such a relationship, we couldn't have cared less.

At some stage, a large percentage of adolescents growing up in Christian homes will utter the refrain "I hate church". This can be for a number of reasons. Firstly, the desire for independence has now stepped up a gear. To headstrong, vacillating adolescents, as good a reason as any for hating church is simply because it is so important to their parents. They can seek to break away from it just so that they can make their own personal choices. It's classic rebel-without-a-cause stuff. You dismiss something in its entirety, purely so that you can then start again and decide for yourself from square one.

Secondly, the adolescent is often ignored in the church context. Many young people feel that the church has mistreated them. I was not an isolated case. Many other young people who have been a little awkward have equally been dismissed for being too high-maintenance. The community of believers needs to learn to handle young people and everything that they bring with them far better than they do at present.

Thirdly, adolescents can claim to hate church because they feel as if they have no place there. For me, this is the most alarming of the three reasons. The other two are short-term problems that can be sorted out far more easily. But this one has no quick fix. Many churches are unable to make young people feel that they have a place. Children are OK, because they are happy to be relatively quiet and fit in. Children can go out to the back to their activities, from where they don't try to influence the "real" church. Adolescents, however, are far more problematic. Their capacity for causing problems is far greater.

Young people unbalance the otherwise settled state of the church community. They often want to do things differently. They have stylistic preferences that can upset the equilibrium. In some local churches, an organ always leads the worship, but many of the youngsters want drums. This causes a real divide. Often it seems that the young people are expected to compromise far more than those who are older. After all, it's been their church for 50 years... The question is, do they still want it to exist in 20? If the older folk in some churches just met the young people in the middle then the future of the church would look a great deal brighter.

Churches need to learn from the mistakes of the past, as this way we needn't miss out on the present and future generations as dramatically as we have done with the last few. For a couple of years, in my work at Youth for Christ, I co-led a gap-year programme called "e.t.a." (evangelism. training. action.) with my wonderful wife, Anne. This was a great experience and it was a real privilege to encounter so many radical young Christian people. We would have a group of around 30 young people aged between 17 and 22, and it was Anne's responsibility and mine to put these people in teams and send them out around the UK to take part in hands-on evangelism amongst fellow young people.

These year-out volunteers were inspirational. They simply wanted to give up a year of their life to serve their peers in the name of Jesus. I often referred to them as a "radical remnant" of young people who wanted to do nothing but serve the King, as that was precisely what they lived to achieve. They had to be a radical remnant: just to have survived in the faith through their teens they had to have been of a certain spiritual calibre. Making it to 18 these days with your faith intact is a far greater achievement than before! The teenager of today faces huge pressures and temptations.

One such young person who came on our year-out programme was a guy named Joel. He was a great young man, and although he could be a bit of a lad he was basically pretty sensible. He was very effective in evangelism and had a clearly infectious way of presenting and living for Jesus within his community. Once he'd finished his year with us he went on to do a theology degree at London Bible College, and has quite a future ahead of him in serving the Lord.

The point of telling you about Joel is not to praise him specifically, but to point out that he also had an older brother. His brother grew up in the same church, around the same people and in the same town. The only real difference is that he wasn't as naturally outgoing, and got left out of things a bit within the church. By contrast, Joel was involved quite heavily in the church, doing things up at the front. Joel's involvement, and the responsibility that came with it, kept him in church meetings where he could grow in the faith. In contrast, his brother was not empowered and believed that he had no reason to be there. He felt like an outsider, got bored, lost interest and left. Today Joel is a budding evangelist, while his brother is nowhere with God.

As the church we must take responsibility for making our young people feel interested, involved and valued. Whether we like it or not, young people are going to struggle within the confines of the church. As teenagers they are going to want to break out and to discover new things for themselves. The problem is not in the struggle, but in how the church chooses to respond. We must not ostracise young people. We need to reach out to them. They need to feel involved and that they are part of a thriving community. This can be achieved in all kinds of ways, from formally in church meetings, through sport, or just in conversation.

When young people say, "I hate church", too often the church responds through their actions as if to say, "Well, *we* hate young people." We need to stem this tide and create an environment in church that is youth-friendly, so that even when young people kick against a wall we still welcome them in with open arms. I recently found myself watching a television programme in which kids can turn the family home into whatever they want to whilst their parents are away. How would adults feel if young people did this to the church? This would seem like the end of the world for many churchgoers. It highlights the great gap between young people and the church. The desires of young people regarding church are so different, their hopes so dissimilar. As a result they often feel like outsiders.

Young people struggle with what they see in church. They question decisions, are turned off by hypocrisy, and often expect a lot more from the church than is delivered. The disappointing church climate many young people experience is certainly not new. This little story highlights this point well:

A young man named Mark had just become a Christian, so he was looking for a good local church to attend. One Sunday he went along to the church that was situated closest to him, but he was shocked by what he discovered was taking place. It wasn't just the savage gossip that he overheard before the service began – there were plenty of other things going on that he hadn't expected to find. There was the sermon that denied the resurrection of Christ. Then the quarrelling that broke out during Holy Communion, and the group of people who got up and walked out during the prayer time.

After the service, someone took the time to fill Mark in on all the latest gossip about others in the church. He explained how two members of the congregation were taking legal action against each other. He exposed the fact that one individual was carrying on an affair with his stepmother. He also elaborated on the presence of internal strife and party rivalry, and on the way in which the church looked highly likely to undergo a four-way split. In the light of this disconcerting visit, Mark returned home and started to have serious second thoughts about his newfound faith.

Mark's case study does raise some serious pastoral problems for us. It creates questions that are not easy to answer. Is Mark's an isolated experience? Are many churches that vulnerable to a probing, though sympathetic, examination? Perhaps the advice that would most readily be given to Mark might focus on his need to look elsewhere and try to find a different church, to concentrate on seeking out a church more closely modelled on New Testament lines. That advice sounds fine in theory; the only problem is that the church Mark went to was not only patterned on the New Testament ideal of church, it *was* a New Testament church. For Mark was a citizen of the first century, and his local church was the church at Corinth.[4]

Our churches today may not have the same difficulties, but they can be just as ostracising to the young person of the twenty-first century as the church in Corinth was to Mark all those centuries ago.

There is definitely a gap that only a few of us fill, the gap between the wider church and adolescents. I love young people and I love the church and I long to see the two brought together, but at the moment there is a great big gap. I find myself standing in this gap. As someone in the gap, I plead with you to make church a place where adolescents can feel welcome. Create an environment that can live up to the mandate of being the Bride of Christ. Flee from discord, arguments and creating an ungodly status quo. Please make church a place where young people are loved, empowered and blessed. If this is happening in the church and, by association, the home, then adolescents will feel a part of the community and respond positively.

Adolescence is a very difficult time. The last thing that's needed is the church making it harder still. Please go the extra mile; love your young people; provide good role models. Instead of turning them off church by your behaviour or pushing them out through intolerance, please welcome them home!

5 I've Gotta Get Out Of This Place!

A school friend called Tom lived in a massive house not too far from mine and this mini-mansion had a very impressive garden to match. It was huge and provided the venue for many a post-school game of football between a select few others, Tom and myself. I remember very clearly one particular afternoon. Some friends and I were smashing a football around in the early spring sun. While we were all pretending to be playing for England in a World Cup final, Tom's dad was excavating a compost heap with his gardening fork. How lucky we were to be young people of leisure when someone else had to do what looked like hard work.

As Tom's dad continued with his manual labour, all of a sudden a giant rat leaped out of the compost and jumped at his neck. Luckily he had his wits about him and was able to duck the flying rat, which narrowly missed his neck and went shooting off under the fence in search of a more peaceful compost heap elsewhere. The whole thing was pretty shocking. It was over in an instant but we had all been very surprised by the sudden emergence of the flying rat. If a rat feels trapped, it will jump.

The young adolescent, growing up in a Christian home, can sometimes feel like that rat. Young teenagers can easily feel trapped by the confines of what seems like rigid religion. As a young person I often felt this way. I was "made" to go to church every Sunday. I remember resenting this deeply. Like the rat, I wanted to make a leap for freedom – expressed by smoking in the car park outside the building.

I was so angry! Why should I be made to attend a service in which people waffled on about a contrived faith? I was only two months shy of my fifteenth birthday, clearly an adult, and able to make my own individual and informed decisions. If these choices were different from what my parents wanted, then so be it! Besides, I'd been banned from Sunday school, and ever since then my experience of church had seemed anything but positive. If I made it through a Sunday without a complaint of some sort then that was a noteworthy occasion.

Many people were more than happy to remind me that unless I could be quiet I wasn't welcome. Yet I had it quite easy. I met someone recently who was told one Sunday morning after the church service (in which he had behaved impeccably) that if he were to continue wearing his baseball cap to church then he would no longer be welcome. All he had done was sit quietly in a pew during a service, wearing a cap, and yet the church was ready to throw him out. How unbelievably ridiculous! How can we possibly afford such nit-picking? Do we truly desire, as the Body of Christ, to be so shallow and to push young people away because they don't fit in with our narrow-minded and predominantly middle-class views? This rat was getting ever more frustrated and ready to jump!

It is impossible to miss the obvious divide between the will of the parent and that of the adolescent at this stage. The Christian parent who longs for their kid to know the Lord is in the blue corner, while the adolescent who wants to go his or her own way stands defiantly in the red. Inevitably, a time of great difficulty and confrontation lies immediately ahead. In my case, my attitude to it all was never meant as a personal attack on my parents, but the way that I disregarded church attendance with such flippancy could only come across as personal to the parents who drew up the rules. Anything can be seized upon as a reason for missing church or church-related activities, and for me that Sunday-school ban was a convenient pretext.

Unfortunately there is no set pattern that parents can follow on these matters. I have friends who were allowed to choose whether or not they went to church, others who had to go, and some who had a bit of both, and yet there is no clear correlation in my mind (or in the minds of the many folk I've spoken to) about which parental method leads to the most positive response. There is no simple, pithy answer available. Yet one thing is certain: all young adolescents need as much help and support during this period as they've ever done. The world around them is changing at such a rate, and it's essential that the young person be loved and helped along the way.

It is very easy too for parents to become overly defensive. Helen was the mother of Joanna, and one morning they had an argument. Joanna had missed the church youth group the night before and had declared that she felt that the whole thing was a waste of time, and that Jesus probably didn't exist and that if he did then he had just been a "nice" man and certainly not the Son of God. This incensed Helen, who started making it clear to Joanna that none of this was up for debate and that Jesus *was* the Son of God. Whether her daughter liked it or not, she had to accept the truth. Some things in life were simply not open to debate, explained Helen, and her daughter had to understand this.

Joanna's response was inevitable. She couldn't cope with her recently developed ideology being dismissed so easily (ironically the very thing she was doing to her mother's), and so she slammed the door behind her and stormed out of the house. The next morning, Joanna went to kiss Helen goodbye before going to school. Helen dodged and informed her daughter, "No way will I kiss you until you've said sorry." Joanna glared at her mother, picked up her bag and stamped out.

It is vital for the parents to maintain a relationship with the adolescent. Through a relationship, any battle or issue can be faced. If the bond is strong then the difficult teenage years can be survived. However, when the relationship is severed, all is lost. Every little bit of confrontation seems like a war. The problem in the story is that Helen became the adolescent. She resented her daughter's conduct and was prepared to let the relationship break down. Immense difficulty was caused by a battle that wasn't worth fighting.

Parents have to learn to forgive without being asked. This time is hard enough for all involved, without parents making it worse by failing to show grace to the adolescent. The story of the prodigal son is a wonderful biblical illustration of how parents should aspire to respond to their offspring even when they have deeply disappointed, betrayed or upset them. The parable makes it quite clear that, no matter what one's children may do, the arms of forgiveness must always remain open. The prodigal son was happy to be a servant – and was then incredibly surprised by his father's response. If parents respond with unconditional love then this will pleasantly surprise young people.

I used to love helping out a friend who was involved in manual work. I enjoyed it because you could see the end result. Though I'm not incredibly gifted at it, today I like doing the odd bit of DIY around the house. Again, I enjoy seeing the finished product. A great deal of manual labour is worth doing for the end result. The same is true with young people. In the middle of manual work, it's easy to give up. The same applies when investing in young people. However, if you wait around long enough to see the end product, then it is a million times more gratifying than giving up halfway through.

Parenting adolescents requires a major investment of love in spite of the possible pain and difficulty. The dividends of this investment will not be seen until the child is 17 or 18 at the very earliest. Yet the investment is well worth it, as it will reap incredible long-term rewards. These rewards will last a lifetime.

Church can be a huge source of conflict and the young person will often do all they can to fight it. In the mind of the adolescent, everything about church can seem to symbolise enslavement and control. In contrast, the world screams "freedom". Now isn't that ironic! In the absence of a dynamic relationship with Jesus, the cross only offers a load of rules to anti-authoritarian youths. Churches need to remain accessible to young people by being prepared to make the effort that is needed in times of difficulty. If parents and churches can get across to adolescents the amazing relationship of love available in Jesus then the rat won't need to jump. The problem is that too often we focus on the rules.

Most youngsters will want to see how far rules can be bent. One such young person, a lad named Ian, started a relationship with a non-Christian girl. This girl, Donna, meant the world to Ian; she captivated him. One Sunday morning Ian wasn't ready for church. His mum popped her head around his bedroom door and informed him that they would all be leaving for church in ten minutes and that he needed to hurry up. Ian uttered the words that strike fear into the hearts of all Christian parents. For the very first time, he said, "I'm not going to church today." His mum argued with him until it became apparent that he wouldn't be swayed. She said that if this was the case then he must pack his bags and leave the family home. So he did, and he moved in with his girlfriend for six months. Eventually he did return, but the relationships within the family have never been the same again. Communications are strained and Ian doesn't have the slightest interest in Christianity.

What positives if any can be drawn from Ian's story? I struggle to see that any good was achieved. Yes, it hurt his mum that he didn't want to go to church, but how much more did it hurt her to ostracise her son, and cause permanent harm to her relationship with him? When she pushed him away she was only pushing him closer to Donna! Parents must continually look for the positives, no matter how bleak things may seem. They should keep loving, keep communicating and keep praying: knee-jerk reactions can cause immense long-term damage.

What are we really trying to achieve in being dictatorial towards our young people? This is the hardest time for them as well, and it's vital that adolescents are given room to manoeuvre, so they can discover Jesus for themselves. After all, what is genuinely achieved by a young person sitting in a cold church car park, smoking fags Sunday after Sunday?

6   I Need To Fill A Hole!

*T*he philosopher Pascal famously observed that everybody's heart contains a God-shaped hole. What a profound thought! For the teenager there is a basic underlying need for love, acceptance and satisfaction. If this isn't met within the church then the young person will start rebelling against Christianity and ignoring this God-shaped hole. There will immediately be an unavoidable space in his life. As a result he will seek to fill this void with something other than God. After all, God equals church, and church equates to sheer boredom. Why bother filling any type of hole with something that seems like a complete waste of time?

If church consistently fails to scratch where it itches then the adolescent will fill the God-shaped hole with other things instead. The choice of hole-filler will vary greatly depending on the particular young person involved. Hobbies and interests can easily take over, or a different relationship can become "god". I had a friend who was really going for it with God, and was a positive spiritual influence on many of those around her, myself included. Then after a while she went through a patch during which

God didn't quite seem to be as evidently present in her life. He seemed a bit more remote than He had been before. When she worshipped in church, it wasn't quite as exciting as it used to be; Christianity had momentarily lost its edge. As a result she explored other things and slowly started filling her life with the pleasures that the world had to offer. She drifted away and never came back, because she started filling her life with other things and pushed God out.

I still remember very clearly how I deliberately filled my own "God-shaped hole", although at the time the process didn't seem quite so obvious. I was totally dissatisfied with church. I'd seen amazing things in my life, including people getting out of wheelchairs and one leg growing to be the same size as the other in front of my very eyes, and yet the reality of Christian living hadn't quite done it for me. People would never let me just be me; I had to be something I wasn't. I knew God existed and I was pretty convinced by this whole Trinity thing as well. I just didn't want to have to be like most of the Christians I encountered.

This feeling, of being forced into being something that I wasn't, was particularly hard for me. *I was a Christian leader's kid.* Leaders' kids are not often allowed to be just young Christians with their own struggles; they have to be a certain type of Christian. They can often be expected to become "the next whoever", and many older Christians try to encourage this. This whole situation is not always positive. Many people are jealous of, or disagree with, your parents, and the child is caught in the middle.

A lot of people wanted me to be the next Clive Calver. Many had been blessed by his work and, knowing my strong family heritage in Christian ministry, they felt it only right that I should succeed him. I've always looked quite a lot like my dad as well, and this has encouraged those who wanted to see me take on the mantle. The pressure of it all was immense. It seemed as if everyone wanted me to be a little Clive, but I just wanted to be Gav. If I had been left alone to be a young Christian like the rest, then I would probably have coped better. However, if people were going to place too high an expectation on me then that was it. I'd just jack it all in.

It was all so intense. I felt singled out, and often that was just what I was. I remember getting into trouble an awful lot at one particular Christian conference one year, and when the people in charge had to report back to the executive of that conference, the report from the detached youth-work team was particularly interesting. It stated that there had been no real problems at all in that specific year, except for Gavin Calver. It went on to spell out that three weeks on site are no excuse for a filthy attitude and no understanding of how to behave. Now, granted, some of that is factual, but had I not been Clive's boy would the same attention have been drawn to it? Of course not! This theory can be proved by the fact that I spent all my time at that particular conference with two other young guys. They were not mentioned. The only difference between us was that they didn't carry around the burden of being Clive's son, who should therefore know how to behave. I was being singled out. If the Christian world wanted to be like this then frankly it could go stuff itself!

To some of you reading this it may all seem a little melodramatic, and I suppose it can come across as that, but the many other "leaders' kids" that I have talked it over with have found great difficulty in similar situations. My struggles were largely on a national level; others have found it hard in local communities, but either way the fight is on. People have immense expectations of Christian leaders and this can have an adverse effect on their kids. I remember when I was fourteen helping my parents with a family seminar at a conference. There was a time of open questions and the first question I was asked was, "Do you and your brother and sisters fight?" This seems ridiculous, but illustrates the situation. Perfectly sane people viewed us as in some way particularly special and holy. What a complete load of rubbish. Of course we had fights, because we are all ordinary people! Why would anyone assume that, just because my dad speaks on platforms, he or any of his family is any more special and holy than the average person in the pew?

The church has got to learn sooner or later that we are all called to full-time Christian service for the King and that there is no hierarchy within this. Just because some are called to be teachers, preachers and leaders within the church community doesn't set these people apart from the rest. After all, their teaching, preaching and leadership is all just hot air unless the people in the pews respond to it. We need all giftings in order to reach our world for Jesus. We must all work together and feel equally valued in this. The cultivation of the Christian celebrity is so destructive. We all serve the same Jesus.

I remember one year when, as usual, we went on a camping holiday in France. A young lady came over to our tent with her mouth wide open, claiming that she couldn't quite believe that here on the same campsite as her was the real Clive Calver! This incident has since become something of a family joke, but we must take the glory away from the individual. If the focus remains on the person then we are missing the point completely. Not only this, but the pressure on leaders' kids is intensified. In truth, the young lady should have been shocked by the grace of God in allowing my dad to be used so greatly! Instead she was overwhelmed by the presence of a Christian "celebrity".

As a spokesperson for leaders' kids, I plead with you to give them a chance to become the person that they should be, the freedom to develop as best they can and the opportunity to fulfil their own God-given calling. I was never afforded such luxuries and just wish that I had been. Without the freedom to be "Gav" in the Christian community I went off to fill my God-shaped hole elsewhere.

I attempted to fill this void in my life with football (or soccer, for my American friends). It was something that I'd loved since I was a little boy. Gary Lineker's hat-trick against Poland in Mexico during the 1986 World Cup was what really started off the passion. I can still remember the adrenalin flowing through me as he scored his third goal and ran off with both arms (one heavily bandaged) in the air, in sheer jubilation. I recall my six-year-old self leaping around the room; this felt so good. Until my mid-teenage years, football, though very special to me, had only been a pastime. It was something to enjoy and formed an important part of my life, but it never grew out of proportion. Now things were different.

Now I needed to try something new and see how that fared in comparison to religion, which I saw as having stung me. Some would have tried drugs but I didn't need to, because football was my drug. In football I found an identity; I was someone; I could have real value. As a result I had a sense of belonging, out of which came purpose. I was finding in football everything that seemed to be lacking in church.

With football subconsciously established as my new deity, I had to find more time for it. I started playing in lots of matches, training a great deal, and watching any football that was readily available, be it live at the ground (when finances permitted) or on television. Hand in hand with my new lifestyle came a change in priorities.

The names of the twelve disciples were no longer important and instead it was the names of the eleven who won the 1966 World Cup that now mattered. The Bible was replaced by *Shoot* magazine or any sports pages from a newspaper as the compulsive reading of the day. The Ten Commandments were replaced with a new (far simpler) list of five: 1) You must support your local team (included in this was going to watch their games at the stadium and wearing the team's colours); 2) You must play in as many games of football as possible, be they serious or not; 3) You must

know every footballing statistic that is of any importance whatsoever (for some reason this was never
compared to trainspotting); 4) You must defend your
team in public no matter what, and against whatever
criticism deluded lower life forms may choose to
offer; and 5) You must be filled with hopeless optimism every summer that this time the team you play
for, as well as the one you support, really *will* win the
league.

I played football an awful lot. I played for my
school, for local teams (both full teams and five-a-
side) and in any park kick-around that was available.
After a while I realised that I was actually quite good
and so I began to do specialist one-on-one football
training with a coach as well. I was a goalkeeper and
was as cocky as any young lad would have been. At
around this time I was probably spending about 80%
of my leisure hours on football. From reading the latest football news on Teletext to playing Subbuteo, my
life became one long obsession with a game whose
origins involved a load of men running all over the
place after an inflated pig's bladder.

The obsession grew. With every trophy I won, the
desire became stronger. I was convinced that I would
be the next great 'keeper, and that one day I would be
paid for my obsession. With hindsight I know that I
was good, but never quite that good. Despite my great
desire to play the game, what I really adored – and
the thing with which I tried to fill my gaping cross-
shaped hole – was watching live professional football
and following it in the media. My primary passion
was going to watch my beloved Wimbledon Football

Club. I'll never forget my first ever match. I went with my dad and big sister, Vicky. Wimbledon were playing Arsenal and, despite trailing them 2–0 at half-time, they came back to win 3–2, scoring the winning goal with 30 seconds left. It was an incredible moment: at the age of eleven I had fallen in love.

Supporting Wimbledon was heaven. As a teenager, I was truly free only on the terraces at Wimbledon. It was the one place where I felt no burden of expectation. I could be anonymous in an environment that I was desperate to be a part of. I felt no need to rebel, as I was part of a community. We were heading in the same direction. It's easy to go with the flow when your lives and destinies are so mutually entwined. If Wimbledon won, we would all celebrate. If they lost, we had one another for support in our mourning. For the first time I experienced what I perceived to be true freedom and happiness.

Being part of a community of football supporters wasn't that different from going to church. The same optimistic and faithful remnant would turn up each week without fail. Within the group that gathered on the terraces were the usual characters, just as there were in the church hall sipping coffee every Sunday morning. Included in this group were the people who remember the "good old days" when everything was perfect and who hankered after a return to such times. So too were there those who had to seek attention by being very vocal, who were desperate to be heard: no matter how trivial the issue, they had a view on everything! Finally, in both establishments there were those who were utterly convinced that everything had to change immediately or there was surely no point in carrying on.

The subject of worship also threw up striking resemblances. Now this was uncannily similar. Communal singing, in which adoration was poured onto the players on the pitch, was the order of the day. The crowd had their favourite songs, which they would sing with extra gusto, just as those in church do when they sing their favourite hymns. I was from a charismatic background, and it seemed even more like church when the arms went up in the air and people closed their eyes at particular heart-rending moments. This belief in football certainly seemed as authentic as any faith in Jesus.

I was happy to commit to this footballing thing for life. I was a regular at Wimbledon throughout my teens and became more and more convinced that this was to be my spiritual home. I threw so much of myself into supporting the team that a spiritual home was just what the stadium became. Following this team of eleven men with commitment and devotion was fundamentally a spiritual exercise. There was an advert for televised football on billboards that said that 90% of males were worshippers of eleven men on a grass pitch. I was one such worshipper.

Wimbledon were known as The Wombles, and one song that we used to sing on the terraces stated that we were "Wombles till we died". I particularly liked singing this one and would belt it out, as I wanted this football team to be everything in my life. This football team would not let me down in the way that the church had. This team never promised anything; they just provided hope of a better day when they might win something. They weren't deluded about an afterlife; it was just a case of living for today. This team never said one thing and then did another, as Christians seemed to do. This deity was not about a rulebook but instead all about hope, dreams and adrenalin.

I'd finally found my religion. I was going to keep playing as much football as possible, and would follow Wimbledon with everything in me. I'd filled my God-shaped hole. I'd picked my path in life. Forget this Christianity rubbish; I knew what I was living for. I was to be a Womble till I died!

7   I'm Still Not Happy!

*I*t was a chilly January afternoon. I was full of great hope and expectation as I ran from the classroom in pursuit of the train that would take me home. Double science had dragged on and on and I had counted the minutes till the final bell that signalled freedom to this desperate fifteen-year-old. I'd just about managed to keep myself entertained by drawing up football teams in the back of my science book. Things like the greatest team of bald footballers or the best team of overseas players to have played in Britain ever: I'm sure you get the general idea. Now finally it was all over and I was determined to get home as quickly as was physically possible. The mundane process of photosynthesis could be left behind in favour of far higher things. After what had seemed like an eternity I was freed from my classroom cell.

As I continued running towards the railway station I could feel the adrenalin pumping through my veins. This was the day that I'd been waiting for. I'd lost an awful lot of sleep over the imminent events of today and had been focusing all my best energies on its outcome. Why was this night so important?

Wimbledon had made it to the semi-finals of the League Cup and the second leg of this was to take place on this very evening. We were only hours away from a trip to Wembley Stadium!

I'd been faithfully watching every Wimbledon home game for six years now and this was the moment that I had been waiting for. I would have to be at my best. If I could muster up the energy to sing every song as loudly as possible then I was utterly convinced that this would make the ultimate difference to those eleven men running around in the name of Wimbledon on the football pitch. Tonight would finally be the night when we would make it to a cup final, and I for one had been filled with butterflies all week long. This was to be our moment, the climax of our achievements. By the end of this night we would be in football heaven.

Despite the fact that the game wasn't due to start for over four hours, I was in such a rush to get home because I desperately needed every extra moment possible in order to go through my essential preparations before the game began. Nothing could be left to chance. I finally rounded the last corner and made it to the station just in time to leap onto the train as the doors shut sharply behind me. What a relief it was to make it onto that train, as the next one wasn't due for another 20 minutes and I could ill afford to waste that time standing on a station platform on a day like this.

Two stops later we finally pulled in to my home station of Forest Hill and I leaped off the train and made the short dash home in as short a time as possible. I wasn't going to waste any time now. Once I'd reached the front door of my house I opened it with such haste that it must have seemed as if I were being chased by a large pack of dogs. I ran upstairs to my room and began my pre-game routine. I got my Wimbledon top out and laid it on my bed with my matching hat and scarf. I was so proud of the blue and yellow colours of Wimbledon. The shirt, hat and scarf looked great when I wore them together. I then grabbed the video of highlights of some of Wimbledon's greatest goals and put it on. The memories came flooding back as I watched my heroes celebrating an endless collection of magic moments. My mind drifted to the video that would inevitably be produced from tonight's game; imagine how special *that* will be, I thought. This truly was to be our year.

When the video had finished I filled my time with whatever triviality would help it pass until I was called down for dinner. During the meal I was unusually quiet. Often I would talk a great deal at mealtimes but today I simply had to concentrate on that which really mattered. My knife and fork were slipping out of my hands, which were sweaty with anxiety. I felt that I might pass out. I usually ate a great deal, but tonight I barely touched my food. My mind was entirely elsewhere; I was focused, and I was in the zone.

Shortly after I had finally been excused from the dinner table in order to get on with what were clearly more important things, my dad arrived home. He wanted to wait for a while but under my constant badgering he finally agreed to go to the stadium now.

I simply had to be at the ground, surrounded by like-minded people with whom I could live out this dream. I was kitted out and ready; Dad was nervously excited and we were raring to go. It didn't mean quite the same to him but he was very keen nonetheless. He was often pessimistic about our chances but on this occasion we were united in hope: after all, it wasn't Manchester United that we were playing, only Leicester City!

The first leg of the semi-final had been played at Leicester City's ground at Filbert Street, and we had drawn that game 0–0. The stage was set for what was sure to be an incredible night. We eventually arrived through the traffic and parked in the usual area near the ground. As we approached my temple of worship I could sniff victory. We always did well against Leicester and this year we had the best team of players that I could remember, a real collection of top-notch talent. Even the nostalgic guy who sat near us every week, convinced that the golden era of Wimbledon had departed 25 years ago, admitted that this year's side were good. Six international footballers playing in the same team for Wimbledon was totally unheard of.

Dad would always buy me a programme, as I earnestly collected them. I remember realising that I must keep it extra safe and in good condition, as tonight we were making history. Just as my dad and I were experiencing this together, so too one day I would show the programme to my son and talk him through this momentous occasion in Wimbledon's history. My future son would listen to me time and again explaining every minute detail of this glorious evening. He'd be a Wimbledon fan too; it's in the genes!

We shifted from the programme seller and into the queue to get inside the ground. There was a real buzz about. We finally made it through the turnstiles and headed towards our usual seats in the home grandstand. We had season tickets at Wimbledon and our seats were in the front row, just to the left of the goal.

It was comforting to know that we were in familiar surroundings, amongst the usual people. The nostalgic guy; the gentleman I sat next to who was very educated in the game; the young lady who sat behind us and was always so nervous that she didn't really watch; the fat bloke who always wore no top to the game, no matter what the weather (and who had *Womble till I die* tattooed across his chest) – the list went on and on. We were all in it together, and would share the joy.

In spite of the familiar faces around I was desperately agitated and couldn't get comfortable as I fidgeted in my seat, anxious for the action to begin. Eventually, after what had seemed like an age, the game finally started. All began well. Dad and I joined in a chorus or four and I was totally confident. Dad was as ever surprised at how the fans had found out such intimate details about the referee's personal life. After 23 minutes of play the amazing happened: a Wimbledon striker called Marcus Gayle had seemed to be going nowhere when suddenly he hit a very ambitious shot that fizzed into the corner of the net.

Wimbledon had scored a goal! We were on our way. Wembley, here we come! We danced, sang and laughed our way to half-time. This was surely to be the best moment of my life so far.

Dad and I had a half-time drink together and were elated as we made our way back to our seats. The whole place was buzzing. The second half started and we were belting out songs of adoration from our end of the ground. From the noise that the Wimbledon fans were making you could have been forgiven for forgetting that there were any Leicester fans in the ground at all. We weren't known for having many fans, but tonight the place was full and we were making a deafening sound. Time was moving on nicely and our cup final was getting closer and closer with every breath. Yet my joy was turning to anxiety as every moment passed. Each second began to feel like a minute and every minute like an hour. I was totally desperate for this game to end.

Then, like a bolt from the blue, the unthinkable happened. From a floating corner, Leicester scored. There were only thirteen minutes of the 90 left. I couldn't believe it! The whole ground fell silent. In a confined space filled with thousands of people you could have heard a pin drop. The whole place was stunned! But it wasn't over yet. After a few moments of silent disbelief the crowd were roused once more and we sang with all that we had left in the vain hope that our team might score just one goal. Somewhat inevitably, they didn't, and when the final whistle went we knew that the game would go to 30 minutes of extra time. This additional time flew by and with every second that passed the anxiety grew. We had to win this specific game, otherwise Leicester would go through to the final, because they had scored at our ground (commonly known as an "away goal").

With just two minutes left, my boyhood hero (a footballer called Robbie Earle) jumped up high and headed the ball towards the goal that we were sitting behind. Every person in the ground was sure that we'd scored again and the Wimbledon fans had already begun celebrating. I could feel myself rising to my feet; we'd done it; we were going to a cup final! Then to our utter dismay the ball hit the inside of the post and bounced back out. It wasn't a goal. That was it, surely. I sank back into my seat, feeling betrayed by the man who had been my hero for so many years.

Two minutes later the game was over and it was Leicester City who would be going to Wembley to play in a cup final. Wimbledon would get nothing. I couldn't believe it: how had this happened? We'd lost. Everything in me had told me that this was impossible. My deity had failed me. I'd given everything to this football team and in turn they'd let me down. This God-shaped hole that had felt so full suddenly gaped wider than ever. Wimbledon was the last thing in my life that I had expected to be so unfaithful to me. I spent the next few days in complete desolation. For someone who's usually very loud, I hardly uttered a word over the next three days. I couldn't cope with what felt like the ultimate betrayal.

The attempt to fill my God-shaped hole with football had failed. It had worked for a while, but that semi-final against Leicester City had shown how temporary this satisfaction was. With hindsight it all seems so simple: no one other than God can fill a God-shaped hole. However, at the time it's not so easy. Dissatisfaction with Christianity leads to a pursuit of other things, which offer short-term benefits but will eventually leave you empty again.

For young people from a Christian home the whole thing is very hard. They have experienced at least a little of the eternal truth of Jesus. As a result there is often a perpetual nagging in the back of their minds about this, and a need to reaffirm it in their own lives, which is all very difficult and makes life quite taxing. It is also hard if a young person has tried to find fulfilment elsewhere, and failed. To admit that Christianity is the way to go takes a great deal of humility and maturity. Such characteristics are often not readily available at this age. I know that the need to humble myself and admit that I was wrong delayed me in my walk with God by at least a couple of years. I simply didn't want to face up to my mistake. I couldn't handle all those snotty Christians reminding me that they had told me so.

Those who pursue other things in order to fill their God-shaped hole may struggle to ever turn back. Football soon let me down, and as such it was easy to discard. However, for those who fill their God-shaped holes with things such as drugs and sexual immorality, the whole thing can be a great deal tougher. Such vices bring with them subcultures that are hard to break out of.

The consequences too can be a great deal more serious: all-consuming drug addictions; unwanted pregnancies; sexually transmitted diseases. As a result the church devastatingly and needlessly loses many young people. The church needs to make it easy for youngsters to return after having messed around. The church *must* be gracious in welcoming prickly teenagers back. It's hard enough for young people to humble themselves and come back without the church making it even more difficult.

My dad stuck by me through my football phase. It was something that we really enjoyed together. Parents need to understand what their child is infatuated with and help him or her through it where possible. If the parent understands the young person and a bit of his or her world, then they can help a great deal more effectively when it all goes wrong.

For all that the church and parents can do, we need to be clear about the fact that a personal relationship with Christ is the only way to fill a God-shaped hole! The statement "I'm still not happy" will be continually uttered, be it consciously or subconsciously, until the Lord is allowed to take His rightful place and fill the voids in our lives.

8 Why Can't I Be A Christian Without The Church Bit?

*T*he church doesn't come across as being very youth-friendly. The worship, format of events and preaching are all aimed at the core group – the middle-aged, the old and young families. The young person seeking to be an adult is often left out. Churches are very good at children's work but I remain to be convinced that they are all that good at youth work. Yes, we're good at doing missions and reaching out to those outside, but do we really make it attractive to those on the fringes?

Ask yourself: what is there in your church that would particularly appeal to a teenager? Often there's not an awful lot. We too often just expect young people to get on with it and keep quiet. We hope that they will dress appropriately and never want to change the way that *we* like doing things. We dream of their finally being convicted about wearing ripped jeans and having multiple body piercings. Surely such dress is inappropriate? Essentially we long for young people to be sensible conformists. How very boring!

Such views need to change if we hope to have a

church with a bright future. We can't afford such prejudices if we are to move forward. When he was 16 my brother Kris was quite a picture. He wore jeans with so many rips in them that there was little material left, had his ears pierced, grew his hair long and looked like an all-round young rocker. My mum remembers one occasion when she was at a conference and Kris was working at that time as a platform steward in the big top. It was the final morning of the week and he was busy on the stage setting things up for Communion. He was just going about his business when my mum walked in to the back of the tent and saw him on the stage. With embarrassment, she later admitted to me that she hoped no one would make the association between them!

Parents need to accept their children and not be ashamed of them. Kris didn't look the part, and in Christian families as well as the church as a whole that seems to matter far too much. Why? It's only with young Christians that it seems to matter. People claim to want youth in the church, but half the time it seems that what is really wanted is a load of younger-looking but essentially middle-aged clones who won't rock the boat.

Youth are totally welcome so long as they don't upset the status quo. A number of people have been going to the church since before these youngsters were born, and therefore they feel they have the right to decide how it runs. Such attitudes are ridiculous, as they only work for the next 20 years or so. After that point there will be no church left to say that "We've always done it this way". The church in much of the West will have died. As a man in his twenties I'm not prepared to let this all go unchallenged: I don't want to be meeting on my own in the future. My peers need to know Jesus and the church needs to welcome them in no matter what they look like, smell like or have pierced!

It is out of this general church climate that things such as youth churches have emerged. I really struggle with the concept of "youth church". Having a word before "church" that suggests a minority group seems totally wrong to me. I can't process it at all, as my understanding is that *all* ethnic groups, genders and ages should meet together in our Father's house. Therefore, in and of itself the whole concept of youth church seems fundamentally flawed. But, then again, doesn't the idea of the current, predominantly middle-aged church seem just as daft?

I remember discussing the whole topic of youth church with a friend of mine called Andy, who's a pastor of a youth congregation in the north of England. We had quite a heated theological debate and eventually came to the same conclusion: that "youth church" falls outside the biblical ideal of church. However, Andy did make a very poignant comment. He said, "What am I supposed to do – run a youth church that isn't theologically ideal and have a load of young people in my church, or stick to my theological principles and let them all have no place in which they can express their faith?" It's quite a predicament, isn't it? In the end we have to be realistic, and Andy and I agreed that we would rather be answerable to Christ about a theological misnomer than about letting the young people of a town go to hell whilst we remained in our Christian ivory towers. Yet it's a sad indictment that the church today is so unfriendly and irrelevant to youth that we are pushed into a corner in which "youth church" becomes the only viable pragmatic possibility.

Fundamentally, most pastors are pragmatists more than they are theologians anyway. The gut-wrenching thing is that in their heart of hearts these pastors don't value youth. As a direct result we are pushed into a theological debate on youth and children's church instead of being practical. On so many other issues pastors don't seem half as determined to stick to theological principles.

I remember as a teenager desperately wanting to give the faith a go but always feeling held back by the constraints of the church. If I could have been a Christian without the burden of church then I think I might have jumped at the possibility. I went to what was deemed a youth church, but the problem was that it wasn't that at all. It was one of the earliest forms of this type and essentially it was a normal church, just with a different name and tie-dyed sheets on the ceiling. There was no more freedom there than anywhere else. People were just as judgemental. The leaders still had their favourites and it took only about 30 minutes for whatever misdemeanours had taken place there to be retold to parents over the phone. Ours was a junior version of the larger model. It wasn't aimed at us. Just because it was on Wednesday and Friday nights instead of Sunday mornings wasn't enough to make it different.

The leader still had a go at me for the same things that my parents did. More young people participated than at "real" church, but even then they were given a very tight brief and watched as if by hawks. There was a select group of people who took part and this was the same no matter what. I've gone on to preach on platforms all over the UK yet in "my" youth church I was never asked to do anything. Not even to put the songs up on the overhead, say a short prayer or (if I had been particularly fortunate) read a scripture. I suppose they thought I wasn't up to it. Talk about empowerment! All the things that I hated about adult church seemed even more apparent here. The truth is, it was a hundred times more annoying, as at least in the big church they didn't pretend to be anything that they weren't! Here they claimed to be for the youth yet what I was experiencing was quite the opposite.

It breaks my heart to think of the potential that was lost as a result of the way that that youth church was run. We would have been better off staying in the adult church where no false promises were made and where our expectations were understandably lowered. At least then we didn't feel so left out because it wasn't a small group of peers who were singled out as the only ones worthy of participating, but instead a clearly defined remnant of people our parents' age.

However, this is an unduly negative picture to draw from youth church overall. Some youth congregations are bursting at the seams, incredibly evangelistic and empowering. Invariably such congregations have been shaped by the youth themselves. They have been responsive. These youth churches have found freedom of expression, which has led to things being conducted in a multitude of ways. A guitar (let alone an organ) doesn't always lead the worship and there isn't always a preacher. Parents aren't phoned when youths are "naughty" and young people are treated far more like adults. I came across one such church and was deeply encouraged by it. I went there to speak and the young people were very responsive. They had freedom to interact and shaped the church themselves. The leaders had spiritual authority but they combined this with wisdom and empowered their congregation. Spiritual authority after all is about the empowerment of others, not the caging of them.

Having been there myself I could always empathise with the person who'd been outside smoking during the sermon instead of inside listening with the others. I always felt an affinity with such people and because of this it was he whom I went to find after the service. I knew exactly who he was; I'd seen him walk out the minute I'd been invited up to speak. As I went to speak to this guy I noticed that the pastor was already there. He wasn't telling him off either. They were chatting about football results and were getting on well, the guy talking very warmly with the pastor. He was made to feel totally welcome and a part of it all even if he chose to stand outside.

I asked the pastor about it and he said, "What good is it leaving him out because he doesn't like sermons? I love the guy and want to see him give his life to the Lord. Six months ago he didn't come in for the worship time and now he does. We're making real progress with him and nothing could be further from my mind than making him do things he doesn't want to do. I believe in prayer and I pray for him every day. The Lord's in control and this guy's warming up to the message."

What a contrast this was to my experience. As a result of this approach the youth church in question is holding on to a number of its people. When they get to the age of 18 (19 at the most) they are fed into local churches. The local churches run the youth church together, and as such everyone works for the greater good. These churches can see the huge benefit, and as a result contribute financially towards a full-time worker and the hire of a building. This ecumenical vision has meant that all of the churches involved are now reaping the rewards of the venture, with far more young people in their churches than they had before they started the youth congregation five years ago.

People have to leave at 18 so that the youth church remains just that – a place for youth. Youth churches have been a pragmatic solution but they must always remain a very short-term one. Many other youth churches have tended to develop first into a young-adult church and then into a young-families church. This process goes on and on, so that within that particular church there is only really one subculture represented. This is the problem if there is no cut-off point at which youth must be fed in to the wider church. With the climate in which the church exists we can no longer afford any level of segregation. For the sake of our corporate future we need to work together. There need to be all different types of people, ages, races, backgrounds and classes sat side by side in the pews.

Youth church should always recreate itself for the next generation. No generation is the same and so there must be continual evolution in order to reach and keep as many young people as possible. We have to do everything in our power to witness to teenagers, as time is running out. Many youth workers don't hang around for all that long because the process of adaptation is so draining. We need to support youth workers through this process. There must be fluidity and flexibility as we reach young people. Our substance never changes – we are based on the revelation of Christ – but our style must change. Youth work should be responsive to its surroundings. If young people skate in the town, then how does the local church work with skaters? If there is nothing to do locally, what can the church put on? We must constantly remake ourselves in order to save young lives. The process is exhausting but it's well worth it.

The integration of young people from youth church into wider church must take place on all levels and not just on those that the rest of the church is comfortable with. Many churches may be thriving right now, but they're dying in their comfort, because the average age of church members is rising every year. If we want young people in the pews then there has to be give and take. They need to be in the church for good, and if we are to achieve this then we have to work at making them accepted and welcomed.

Unfortunately, my youth church did it differently. It breaks my heart to think how many of my mates were lost along the way. Of a friendship group of ten to fifteen people, only one other and myself are still going for God today, just eight to ten years on. A lot of those around me who packed it all in claimed to be disappointed with Jesus, when really they were disappointed with church. The two had become synonymous with one another. The whole situation makes me feel sick, because if things had been done differently who knows what might have happened?

Yet in spite of the many negative stories you may hear (including my own in this chapter) and the flow of depressing statistics, we must not give up. We may be running out of chances, but there is still hope. We can still win young people for Christ; we can still give the church an exciting future; we can still reverse the statistics. My few years at Youth for Christ have instilled eternal hope in me for the young who are lost; there *is* still time. The church has a great opportunity to learn from its mistakes and build for the future. But we have to choose to learn.

Youth churches can work very well, and they can just as easily do the opposite. We must endeavour to help young people to integrate into church whilst realising that faith is fundamentally based on a relationship with Jesus. Church may seem like everything to you but you won't have the protection of its four walls when you face your Maker head-on. Church is incredibly important but its rules, politics and forms of worship will all be left behind when we die. What we take with us is our relationship with Jesus.

Like many of my friends I was certainly disappointed with church, though I said it was with Jesus. It wouldn't be all that long until I worked out the difference. Tragically, an awful lot of my peers didn't hang around long enough to work it out.

9 My Parents Are Trying To Do It For Me

R ebecca is from a Christian home. She grew up with the usual things involved in growing up in such an environment: Bible stories; Sunday school; summer camps; youth club – I'm sure you get the general idea. Despite all of this she had never taken this Christian thing very seriously, and even the most optimistic of believers could only really describe her faith as nominal. She was happy with this. She could go along with the Christian thing when it suited her best and could equally alienate herself from Christianity completely when that fitted her agenda better. Rebecca enjoyed juggling issues of faith and any association she might choose to have with them.

On her fifteenth birthday she had been given a CD by a Christian band and had somewhat reluctantly listened to it. It was actually quite good; in fact she really enjoyed it. She looked through the album sleeve and to her astonishment the band all seemed pretty cool as well. The lead singer was well fit, she thought. She showed it to her friend Jill, who agreed that the singer was quite a looker, and the two of them decided that they would go and hear the band live. About two months later the band were playing at a Christian outreach event locally and so Rebecca and Jill set off together. Apathetic though Rebecca was about everything Christian, she was very excited about the night ahead because she really did enjoy their music (and had grown to adore the singer's chiselled features).

The band were great that night, far better than they sounded on the album. Rebecca loved the set they played and she loved the lead singer even more. He was truly drop-dead gorgeous. When the band's electric set had finished, a speaker came up to the stage. As on similar occasions this seemed to be Jill and Rebecca's cue to go outside. This time something different seemed to be happening, and the speaker seemed strangely alluring, so Rebecca stayed even though Jill left.

Sure enough the preacher said some things that resonated deeply within Rebecca. She felt herself incredibly moved by what was said. All of the Christian theory that had been spouted at her for years seemed to be making sense. This Jesus was real; He had died on a cross; He loved her and she truly did need to welcome Him into her life. This seemed to be a great turning point. "Nothing need ever be the same again," said the speaker, and tonight for once she shared the sentiment. This God thing *was* for her. What she had always heard said around her would now become truth in her life.

Rebecca was going to give this Christian thing one great big try, and she decided that she had to let those people around her know all about it. She told Jill later that evening. Unfortunately for Rebecca, this information was neither here nor there to her friend who'd grown up in a Christian home, had heard it all before and wasn't fazed by any of it. Disappointing as this was, Rebecca wasn't knocked; she knew that it would be very different at school on Monday.

That had been the Saturday night and now it was Monday morning and time for Rebecca to go to school. As she left her house there was a strange feeling inside her: this was the first day that she would go to school as a Christian. What a great witness for Jesus she would be in her playground. With a spring in her step she set off, anxious to begin this new-found role.

She was about to turn the final corner before school when she bumped into two of her good friends, Tania and Kate, who were smoking and discussing the boys that they had "been with" that weekend. They offered her a fag and to their utter astonishment she turned it down. What was going on? Rebecca smoked 20 a day, after all. Tania was the first to comment: "What's wrong with you? You're always up for a smoke." Rebecca replied somewhat sharply, "I don't smoke any more. I'm a Christian now." Simultaneously they both gulped down too much smoke and started coughing. "You *what*?" bleated Kate. "You've become one of those Bible people?" "Yes," replied Rebecca. The two other girls gave her one last look of disdain and walked away. They were no longer interested in their "friend".

This wasn't going to knock all of the enthusiasm out of her, thought Rebecca, unaware of the fact that this was just the beginning of the struggle. The rest of the day went from bad to worse, and by the end she had decided that enough was enough and she gave up on her short-lived faith.

Meanwhile, her parents had spent the whole of that day excited by the news of their daughter's decision. They had told every Christian friend and relative that they could think of. They'd been worried about Rebecca for a while now and the great corporate sigh of relief breathed by Mum and Dad on that day could be clearly sensed by all with whom they chose to share what they perceived as such great news. Little did they know of the day that their daughter had faced, or the subsequent decisions she had made. The battle most certainly was on.

Oblivious to her daughter's day, Mum stopped off at the local Christian bookshop on her way home from work. She was going to buy her daughter a Bible. One of those "youthy" ones, thought Mum, as she picked a gaudily coloured Bible off the shelf. Rebecca will love that one, she mused. Mum was so excited as she handed it over to her daughter. To her amazement, the gift was rejected. Rebecca explained the situation and made it clear in no uncertain terms that she had no interest whatsoever in the book. Parental ecstasy had turned to agony in the blink of an eye.

Mum and Dad were horrified and struck by a sudden realisation that they didn't know what on earth to do next. They couldn't face losing their daughter from the faith. Dad backed off somewhat, which infuriated Mum. To compensate for what she saw as her husband's apathy, Mum decided to do quite the opposite. She would fight for her daughter's faith. Over the next few weeks Mum certainly did put up a very brave fight.

She was relentless in her efforts, and no amount of apathy on Rebecca's part could quash any of her enthusiasm for the task in hand. Mum did all that she felt she could to live her daughter's faith for her. She brought her Bible notes, left books on her bedside table, brought God into every single conversation, insisted on saying grace for every snack (though she did stop at individual sweets), and so on.

The biggest problem was that the more Mum tried to push Rebecca towards Christianity, the more anti-Christian Rebecca became. There was a clear correlation between Mum's tireless efforts and Rebecca's antagonistic views towards the faith. The wedge between them was growing rapidly. Mum was becoming somewhat exasperated by it all, and Rebecca was getting a warped sense of achievement in continually rebuffing her mum's efforts. She was in a worse place spiritually after her brief flirtation with Christianity than she had been before.

The devastating thing is that all this happened ten years ago, and to this day Rebecca hasn't come back to faith and has remained vociferously anti-Christian in her comments, world view and lifestyle.

It is very easy to understand why parents try to live their kids' faiths for them, yet this approach doesn't work. Young people can be encouraged towards faith but over the long term no degree of forcing them will be successful. Yes, you might feel better about their regular attendance at church, but sooner or later most of them rebel.

Nevertheless, there is hope. Young people pick up on the example of those around them. This appears to be the best model. Young people see how their parents live and this has a profound influence. The effects may kick in straight away or might take 30 years to come into force, but your parents' example is very hard to shrug off. If you've witnessed those whom you love living a faith and not just speaking one, then these memories stay with you.

Most parents are great with their children up to the age of thirteen. After this point they become overly protective and this process intensifies as the young person grows into later adolescence. The church is often hopeless here as well. During my time running a gap-year programme I came across many over-protective parents who just didn't get it. I would speak to them on the phone about their child's taking a year out and get lambasted for stopping their child from going to university. These Christian parents were often more materialistic and upwardly-mobile-minded than those who didn't know Jesus! They had decided their child's future and anything that got in the way of that would receive their wrath.

Once they made it on to the YFC year-out scheme the first term for every volunteer from a Christian home was in essence the same. The young person spent that term battling it out for ownership of his or her own faith. Why did this happen? Well, with all the love in the world, parents try to live their kids' faith for them because otherwise their child might grow up to be a pagan. Many young people have been forced to submit to the gospel. This tactic doesn't work!

Yet for almost all of the year-out volunteers I met, the example of their parents was a key factor. The pressure from home had often been a hindrance when they had lived there, but the experience of witnessing the lifestyle that their parents had adopted was nothing but helpful. Parents need to show that this Jesus is worth living for with every ounce of their being. He is so worth living for that one would die for Him!

The best way to do this is not to force your children to follow Him but to mirror in your lifestyle the esteem with which you hold His example and teachings. The old corny saying that actions speak louder than words is certainly true. The actions of the Christian parent will play a huge role (be it positive or negative) in the spiritual destiny of the child. The balance between the parent who is too pushy and the one who is a good role model is a very fine one. It's incredibly hard to get it right, and I envy no parent in struggling with this, but we must find avenues through which our youth can fully own a personal faith. A purely inherited faith is not worth a great deal when the going gets tough, but a personal faith is the making of an individual.

It's usually OK for those who go on Christian year-out schemes because the questioning happens in a setting where it's easy to find the right answers. There are plenty of people around to talk things through with and the pull of the hedonistic secular world is not quite so strong. However, what about all those Christian young people who go away from home for the first time and endeavour to find all of the answers that they require at university? What happens to *them*? It is less of a problem for believers from non-Christian homes. They've already fought many battles. They've had to own their own faith as no one else around them in the home had one. Those from the comfortable Christian homes can often find quite the opposite. They can live off the faith of others.

I never had my own faith as a teenager. In one sense I didn't actually want one, but at the same time the comfortable surroundings of the Christian home often encouraged me not to create one anyway. I knew this Jesus was real. I'd seen too much happen in my time to deny this reality, yet I wasn't that inter- ested in even attempting to follow Him. Part of the problem was that at the time I genuinely felt that amongst the rest of my family there was enough holi- ness to go round. Surely they were good enough to get me in through the back door of heaven? Almost like a "Get-out-of-jail-free" card in Monopoly, I felt that my family had earned enough points to take me with them to heaven.

Then there was the fact that I simply didn't want to go along with what was expected of me. Everyone thought I'd be a good Christian – I was Clive's son; I had the heritage; I had seen things others only read about and was the last person that should question faith. If that was how I was to be seen then I didn't want to go along with any of it. They could all get lost. Why go along with the flow? Must I really be that pre- dictable? I didn't want my whole life planned out for me. I wanted to live a little. Attitudes such as this make the whole thing a great deal more complicated.

If the young person feels that the parent is trying to do it for him or her then the reaction intensifies. The young adolescent desperately seeks to be independent and thus fights against faith. I know that I did, and Rebecca most certainly did. Young people need to have a faith that's worthwhile, and in order to have this they need to develop a personal relationship with Jesus. Parents will consistently, and should always, encourage their kids in faith. However, this encouragement should revolve around loving examples as opposed to overt attempts to live the faith for the child.

In New Testament times a child became an adult at thirteen. The parents went through a process of accepting and allowing this to take place. We don't have an equivalent process today and so even in their mid-twenties a person can still be heavily parented, let alone when they're a teenager. Maybe there is no escaping parents' doing it for their kids to some degree, but young people need to feel that they are free to pursue matters for themselves. Perhaps the church can offer the chance for them to follow things individually by empowering them in youth groups and the wider church, encouraging their thoughts and opinions, and giving them the room and freedom to develop. That way their faith can be meaningful, will be able to grow and will be something that is theirs forever because their parents laid the foundations.

10 Living It Up, Big Time!

Why waste time in arguments when you can be out having fun?

From the young person's perspective, teenage life in the Christian home often seems like one long argument. In clear contrast, the rebellious, self-centred and hedonistic option seems to provide true freedom. In the secular domain people think nothing of drinking ten pints of beer, smoking 20 fags or having a one-night stand. Yet in the Christian home even a minor vocal discrepancy (e.g. a swear word) seems to invoke World War Three. Christian parents seem so pedantic, whilst the secular world is so embracing of all moral choices without thought, regard or comment. The choice is a no-brainer: freedom and fun in the world or restraint and boredom in the church.

It's no wonder the world seems so alluring to the frustrated young person. Why waste time in countless arguments about matters so trivial when you can be out embracing life for all it's worth? Everyone else is indulging in hedonistic pleasure, so why shouldn't the Christian adolescent? If this Jesus does want us to have fun (as he must do), then surely whatever pleasure I can get my hands on is fine by him?

Morality becomes subjective within this cultural climate. In contrast to the somewhat dictatorial Scriptures, in the world, if it's OK by you, then it's fine. Choices become far wider. What Bible to read is replaced with which drink to consume, where to party or whom to sleep with. As for heaven, that changes from an unknown destiny in the very distant future (which possibly doesn't exist anyway) to a truly tangible, alcohol-fuelled night of passion in Leicester Square on a Saturday night. Which seems more appealing? It's no wonder so many young Christians mess around during adolescence.

I've spoken earlier about the place of football in my life, but at this stage it was simply a case of pursuing every available pleasure. One of the main things was, of course, alcohol. Alcohol is so easily accessible and relatively cheap. For somewhere between five and ten pounds you could be away with the fairies within an hour. What a wonderful form of escapism! Alcohol is also a good method of vocalising things that might otherwise remain hidden. If an adolescent has opinions to express, then alcohol provides an inhibition-free environment within which to do it.

My perennial sidekick, Danny, and I were regular teenage drinking partners. We would go down to the off-licence at the end of the road and each buy eight cans of beer for a fiver at least once a week, and often two or three times. We loved doing it, as we had found an affordable and very simple way of having a good time. My bedroom was on the third floor of the house, well away from parents, so we'd take the cans up there and work our way through them as the night went on. As we got older the volume increased. We started buying twelve cans apiece for seven pounds and fifty pence each. The effects were much the same.

As we grew older still, the opportunities expanded drastically. With weekend jobs our financial capacity for drinking increased as well. Now we could drink through 20 pounds or so in an evening. Our options were almost endless. There weren't any places in our area where we couldn't get drunk on 20 quid. That was the whole point; the financial limit for an evening's entertainment was what it cost to get off our faces. The other benefit was that we looked older now. We used to use the same off-licence and, being the taller of the pair, I would go in and stand as tall as I could, speak as deeply as seemed plausible, and buy the drinks. The plan would not work everywhere. In a pub, for example, we would have to sit there in the same building and consume our drinks. The charade was probably not quite perfect enough for us to get away with that. But now we were older. No longer need our drinking be restricted to my bedroom; we were free to push out into public houses and other such venues.

Regardless of the context or amount of drink consumed, I always found drinking to be a great form of escapism. I had been through enough, what with the pressure from home, and only truly felt like myself with a beer by my side and a gradually decreasing consciousness as the alcohol set in. It was the one way in which I felt I could be rid of the need to fight with the issues of faith, which seemed to be increasingly underpinning the whole process of adolescent development. If I could hide away from the true meaning of life behind a few pints of beer then I was very happy to do so. The beer asked no questions. It just tasted nice.

On top of drinking there were always other readily available ways of living it up. Like many normal guys of my age I became infatuated with the opposite sex. I would flit from girl to girl, convinced that the next relationship would be the *one*. If there were women to be had then I'd at least have a good go. I began to see females as trophies, devaluing them on every level. Yet in spite of my rebellious lifestyle I still did not hold with sex before marriage. A combination of understanding God's truth and fear of the wrath of my parents had given me this moral compass. Over time I would become very grateful for this.

Once more I had found what seemed like a foolproof way to avoid the realities of life. If I could find this escape in the arms of a new woman then this would be something that I would quite literally embrace. Blonde, brunette, redhead – if I'm honest, I wasn't too fussy. The women themselves were not so important: the excitement was what mattered. I enjoyed these times, though in the long run they are very destructive. I had to walk with the Lord through an intense process of restoration in order to prepare me for Christian marriage.

For other young people the rebellion revolves around different things. Some will have gone a lot further physically with the opposite (or the same) sex than I did. Others will have become addicted to drugs. Others still may have dabbled in the occult. A heartfelt hope of being different (and of being accepted by their peers) can lead to behaviour of all sorts. Anything not to stand out. Christians are perceived as being incredibly prudish, so rebellious adolescents will fight with everything in them to avoid this.

One reason for such behaviour is the fact that a truly strong relationship with Jesus has not yet developed (the whole issue of faith ownership that we looked at in the previous chapter). One young man, called Robbie, discovered this. He grew up in a Christian home and was well aware of the faith. He could talk you all the way through the Bible and could express parts of it far better than many preachers. However Robbie never really developed an individual faith that he could call his own. What he discovered in the church was inaccurate. Much like the Jews who went on to try Jesus, Robbie saw a system of belief, not a person. The Jewish people missed the Messiah because even while he was there at the end of their noses they were still seeking to complete a religious construct.

Robbie therefore found far greater satisfaction in pursuing the pleasures of the world. Now in his twenties, he comments, "As a teenager, I never knew that this Jesus was about a relationship. It always seemed like a bunch of rules. So I went and enjoyed myself in the world and forgot about the rules. I can honestly say that this was so much better than going to church and following a load of stuffy old rules when I didn't actually know the Rule Maker." Robbie later became a Christian at university, and now says of his faith, "I've finally discovered this relationship and suddenly the world seems to hold less appeal. When I was a teenager I never fully knew this, and so enjoyed the world. It's worth obeying the commands when you get the benefits of the relationship, yet if you take the relationship away then you might as well enjoy yourself."

I can certainly see his point. Many Christian parents are happy for their kids to follow the rules even if they don't yet have the relationship. What we need to do is promote the relationship to all our youth. Without it they may as well enjoy the world, as otherwise they are losing out in both ways! If we promote the uniqueness of Jesus and the fundamental importance of a relationship then we get the whole thing the right way around. If we merely throw the rulebook at people then we might as well give up now.

But we do need rules within the context of relationship. Any relationship of value has rules: friendships; marriages; family. The rules have to be there so that the relationship can work. If the rules are there and the relationship isn't, then what we have is wrong. Rules without a relationship provoke rebellion. Equally, if we have a relationship without rules, we also have a problem. A marriage without any rules or guidelines is destined to fail. Relationship without rules generates anarchy. In Christ we have the opportunity for a relationship and the implications of this are some boundaries. For the relationship to prosper these must be adhered to, but they are never more important than the relationship itself. The rules are the manifestation of the relationship. You don't have to be a faithful husband if you have no wife! We need to get things in the right order. Teach relationship and then the rules can be worked out. Teach the rules, and young people may never make it to the relationship.

When Jesus came to earth he summarised the entire Old Testament Law and the Ten Commandments in just two commands: 1) "Love the Lord your god with all your heart and with all your soul and with all your mind" (Matthew 22:37) and 2) "Love your neighbour as yourself" (Matthew 22:39). If Christians can live up to these then they can develop a relationship with Jesus as well as enjoying the freedom of expression that is found in this. Conversely, if we promote a legalistic form of Christianity then our young people may well run into the arms of the pleasures that the world has to offer instead.

11 America, The Ethiopian Eunuch

*D*ad and I were going out that night. I always enjoyed such occasions because we got on so well, and I was sure that this evening would be no different. It was a chilly winter's night as we strolled to the top of our road. The local pub was my preferred environment and so that's where we went. We found somewhere comfortable and sat down together, indulging in our regular enjoyable conversation. How were Wimbledon getting on? Was John Fashanu really the most underrated striker in Britain? As the conversation moved on, my dad listened intently as I discussed some of my own exaggerated sporting heroics.

Whatever had taken place on the school or community sports field would be retold in the most favourable of lights. I was like a tabloid newspaper: I would "spin" the situation to make it come out just the way that I wanted. Clearly, in my own objective opinion I was the best player in every game that I ever played! Does that sound familiar? We continued chatting about things such as girlfriends and my current social life. Obviously everyone wanted to be my friend and each of the girls in the sixth form had a crush on me! We had always enjoyed each other's company and this night was no different.

Then, all of a sudden, within a matter of seconds, the whole atmosphere between us changed. Dad started talking about something that I simply didn't want to know anything about. He said that he and my mum were being clearly "called" to a new ministry in America. God had allegedly told them that this was the right thing to do, and a number of Christian friends and associates had universally confirmed this. What a load of half-witted religious claptrap, I thought. I simply could not, and would not, believe what he was saying. I was utterly distraught and deeply angry in equal measure. If he was going to keep talking about this nonsense then I was going to stop listening altogether. The whole thing seemed ridiculous. I didn't know whether to laugh or cry so I did neither. I just allowed myself to get more and more angry. The only way that I could show any emotion at this point was through aggression.

I was only 17 years old, not even halfway through my A-levels. How could my parents' moving to America possibly be the best way forward? How was a rebellious teenager even going to begin to understand? What had any of this got to do with God anyway? We kept sitting there with drinks that weren't going down and a distinct lack of communication between the two of us. Every minute felt like an hour as we sat together, both burning with emotion, although for very different reasons. Here was I getting deeply angry and feeling very sorry for myself and yet, at the same time, there was he knowing that

God had said "Go" and yet looking at his son whom he was deeply fearful of losing if he did. What a predicament to find ourselves in!

In the immediate situation, something had to happen. My dad was trying his best to interact with me about it all, but even his greatest efforts were to no avail. By this point I'd stopped listening entirely. I had switched off to everything around me. Like a small child, I seemed to think that if I hid away from it all everything would go back to normal soon enough. My dad continued speaking but as far as I was concerned he might as well have been saying nothing, as no matter what he had said I wouldn't have heard it. I had my head in my hands and as the evening wore on I could feel deep anger welling up inside me. The more time that passed, the greater my rage became. Something had to give. As my dad endeavoured to justify the move still further, it finally all became too much. I looked up for the first time in what seemed like an eternity and made sure that I caught his eye. I had something very important to say.

With eye contact firmly established, I opened my mouth and said, "If a so-called loving God wants to split up our family then he can go and stuff himself." I gasped to take a breath before continuing. "If you move to America then that's it. I won't ever, and I mean ever, live another day as a Christian, or even pretend to be one!" And that was it. I'd said my bit and I threw my head back into my hands knowing that I wouldn't say another word. I'd listened to things that I had no desire to hear and had now pronounced my judgement on the situation. The evening's discussion was well and truly finished.

It was quite clear to Dad as well that the conversation was over. He knew that he wouldn't get another word out of me, besides which he was clearly devastated by what I'd said and not too interested in further conversation either. There was no point hanging around, so we left to go home. The pub was literally three hundred yards from our house and yet suddenly it seemed like three hundred miles instead. That walk home took forever, each step drawn out like a blade. Neither of us had anything left to say.

My mum opened the front door. I spotted a gap, went through it, and rushed upstairs to my bedroom as fast as possible. I'll never forget the look on my mum's face when she opened that door. She had probably been quietly optimistic about the outcome of the conversation Dad and I were having up the road. We were like mates, my dad and I; if anyone was going to understand then that would surely be me. Mum found out all she needed to know from the looks on our faces, any optimism quickly lost as she realised the grief we were both experiencing. As I stumbled up the stairs towards my bedroom, I remember feeling more alone than I had ever done previously. I was utterly desolate! During our time in the pub I'd been far too self-absorbed to take in most of what my dad had said, and it was only later that week that I realised they were flying off to the States for an interview.

My parents returned from the States, and though they shared some of how it had gone, I chose to reflect on the negative aspects in the hope that they wouldn't be offered the position, or even accept it if they were. They knew that they would find out whether they had got it or not on a particular Thursday night in January.

It was a week after the interview, on that very Thursday evening, that I was sitting in a pub with my friends. I knew that tonight was the night and no matter how hard I tried I could never quite get comfortable. It was a pub I was used to, and my best friends surrounded me, yet the anxiety and fear within me meant that I felt as if I was sitting in a dentist's chair waiting for the inevitable drill to come all night long.

I sat in my metaphorical dentist's chair clinging to my dad's mobile phone with sweaty palms. A decision was definitely going to be made that night and, although I didn't want to be at home for it with everyone else, I did want to know as soon as I could. Then the phone rang. With a chill running down my spine I answered it. It was a friend of my dad's, and nothing to do with the situation. I got rid of the friend as brusquely as possible. This was no time for pleasantries. I slammed the phone down. The tension was mounting.

Forty-five minutes and two pints of beer later the phone went again. This time the combination of suspense and fear running through me was almost too much to bear. I felt as if I could pass out at any moment. It was my dad. By the time he confirmed it the news seemed somewhat inevitable: they were to move to America. I slammed the phone down once more, utterly furious. I rushed off to the bar to get the most lethal cocktail of spirits I could find.

After these drinks I was surprised to realise that I wasn't happy. I was completely alone, and as the tearful, insecure teenager that I felt like at the time I phoned the closest thing I'd ever had to a youth worker, a guy called Paul. For someone who considers himself to have a sharp memory, I can remember virtually nothing of that ten-minute conversation. It was just great to have someone to talk to. I'm sure Paul will never know quite how important his counsel was at that very moment.

However, I can clearly recall my response. I would show my parents that they were very wrong. I was going to live it up and prove to them that true fun and satisfaction come from worldly pleasures and not from this Jesus who I used to think existed. I was going to make them regret this decision.

What my parents were doing has a very clear biblical parallel. When Philip was ministering in Samaria (Acts 8:4–8), he was having a great time. Many people were coming to faith, and it was all very exciting. Philip was well known and the idea of leaving such a promising situation must have seemed crazy. After all, "When the crowds heard Philip and saw the miraculous signs he did, they all paid close attention to what he said. With shrieks, evil spirits came out of many, and many paralytics and cripples were healed. So there was great joy in that city" (8:6–8).

Within the goldfish bowl of British evangelicalism, my parents too were well known. They were greatly respected and had achieved a huge amount. Many had come to faith; others still had been deeply encouraged in their walk with God; all in all thousands had been touched in some way. They had "made it", and would be respected and appreciated for the rest of their days. Life could have been quite comfortable from here on. The idea of leaving such a situation behind seemed ridiculous. Starting all over again, in middle age, as nobodies on the other side of the world, was sheer folly. The same could have been said of Philip, though in different circumstances. But despite their success and the apparent stupidity of moving on, both Philip and my parents did just that.

When Philip left Samaria he found himself on the desert road that runs from Jerusalem to Gaza. From a hugely successful ministry situation in the heart of Samaria, Philip now found himself in the middle of the desert. Here, in the desert, he met an Ethiopian eunuch who wanted the Scriptures explained to him. But this was no ordinary eunuch. He was a eunuch in the service of Candace, the queen of Ethiopia. Once Philip had spoken to him this man was converted and baptised. As a result of all this the eunuch then became the first person in history to take the Good News of Jesus Christ to the continent of Africa.

In human terms it would have made far more sense for Philip to stay in Samaria, where things were going well and people were responding. However, God has a far better angle on things than we do, and this often means that He possesses different plans for our lives. By the very fact that He's God, if He says go and it doesn't make sense, then we still need to go anyway as He always knows what is best for His people as well as for the growth of His Kingdom.

In much the same way, my mum and dad left the place where everything made sense and where they had experienced great success. Why did they leave? Because Jesus said so. He's God and His prerogative is to see things that we don't and call us on to the new things that He may be doing.

Although I didn't acknowledge it at the time, this was a hugely significant event in my own walk with God. By moving to the other side of the planet, my parents showed me what really did, and had to, matter. Jesus must always come above everything else in the Christian's order of priorities, no matter what the cost. At the time I hated both my parents and God for this, but it clearly demonstrated to me that this Jesus thing must be pretty special and genuine if they were prepared to give up everything to serve Him. How could two intelligent, articulate and level-headed people make such a move if this Jesus was really only a fabrication of someone's imagination? They were role-modelling Jesus to me through their actions.

Adolescents are desperately searching for authenticity in those around them. Though I was desperately anti-God as a result of my parents' decision, at least I knew that they meant business with this Christian thing. It wasn't just a load of words. They were prepared to act on the truths they proclaimed. This conviction of the authenticity of their faith never left me, no matter how hard I tried to hide from it. It is essential that all Christian parents do their utmost to model to their children that Jesus is the most important thing. Thankfully, for most families this won't involve emigrating to the other side of the world, but it will definitely incorporate the need to show children what truly counts in life.

It may not seem like it at the time, but modelling to your offspring what is worth living for conveys the reality that this Christian thing is of deep significance. This can't help but make an impression on the adolescent who at some point will have to make a decision about whether or not to take on a faith of his or her own. Role models are far more effective than anything else in sharing Jesus with young people. They may not always be available in the home, but the church too can show young people what it is that matters. The church too has a responsibility to demonstrate authentic faith, in order to help raise up a significant generation of young people who live for Jesus above all else.

My parents showed me the importance of following Jesus and that this must be at the core of everything a Christian does. Even though I chose to ignore it for the time being, I noted this in them. It made me respect them more, although at this point that still wasn't enough. They chose to follow God in everything, and move to America. I decided to stay in England, drink a lot and live a little. I was aged 17 and time was running out. Which way would things go? The jury was out and the clock was certainly ticking!

12 Decision Time

*T*his really is it, I thought, as I pulled up at the drop-off point at Heathrow Airport Terminal Three. The whole America thing had seemed completely surreal, and I had half-convinced myself that it would never really happen. That night when Dad had told me about it all had been some six months ago now and the penny was finally starting to drop. My folks really were emigrating to the other side of the globe! Dad had left a few weeks previously and I had been expecting him to return home any moment now, calling the whole move off.

With hindsight, I must confess to being a tad naïve at this stage; this dramatic U-turn was never going to happen. I had to leave my bitter thoughts behind and return to the real world. The traffic sign reminded me that this was a drop-off point, not a parking space. I leapt out of the car, opened the boot and grabbed Mum's suitcase.

Now was the moment we had both been dreading. It was time to say goodbye. Few people enjoy saying goodbye to their loved ones, and this situation seemed more taxing and draining than any previous goodbye I'd ever known. After avoiding the reality that lay before us for what seemed like an eternity, we finally said our goodbyes. As I gave Mum a farewell hug I fought back the tears. I was biting my lip so hard I'm surprised it didn't split in two. She was crying and crying, but I was determined not to shed a single tear, so I bit my lip still harder. I was not going to forsake my masculinity for anything. They were choosing to emigrate to the other side of the world, and no matter what God-speak they might choose to adopt, I was not going to see it any other way. My parents had made a choice and I was not going to express any private pain. Why give them the satisfaction?

As my mum disappeared into the terminal, I realised that I'd succeeded: I'd managed not to cry! For the briefest of moments I was elated by this achievement. I felt, for that short blink of an eye, that emotionally I'd finally become a man. I would be OK in the absence of my parents; I could cope: I was a fighter, a tough guy in full control of his feelings. As quickly as it had come, this brief moment of elation evaporated. Now that my mum had entered the terminal and was finally out of sight, my supposed masculine achievement suddenly seemed meaningless. Why was I so pleased that I hadn't cried? Was it really an achievement at all?

All I had as a souvenir of my parents was a soaked shoulder from my mum's tears, and a car (I'd passed my test the day before and my mum had kindly given me her little Citroën AX). Any brief sense of achievement had been completely drained out of my body. I was no tough man in control of his emotions; I was deeply hurt, and felt like the most solitary person ever. I began to feel more and more upset, and opened the car door to get back in to what now felt like the most depressing of surroundings. This car, which we'd had as a family for the best part of a decade, now contained nothing but my thoughts. No one was coming back and here I was with no sense of whether *I* was coming or going. I never admitted to anyone what happened next. My head sank down to the steering wheel and this 17-year-old lad who thought he was too tough to cry just wept and wept. What was I going to do? Who was I trying to be? The tears continued to flow as my emotions burst out in an uncontrollable wail.

Why couldn't I show my mum that I was hurting too? This is one of the main difficulties for the adolescent male. He doesn't want to show weakness, or indeed any outward sign of emotion. The last person to whom a young man will choose to expose what he regards as emotional weakness is his mother.

There was a sudden thud on the car window, and I looked round to see a big burly security guard yelling at me to move out of my drop-off car parking space. I felt like getting out of the car and smacking him in the face. On swift reflection I decided against this plan of action, because he knew nothing of what I was going through (and he was far bigger than me). Instead, I drove off.

I remember virtually nothing of the journey back across London. I suppose I was just anaesthetised. In due course I drew up at my new residence. It was a great house, belonging to a lovely couple from the local church called Rob and Pat, from whom I had rented a room. Both Rob and Pat were out at work when I got back from Heathrow, and as I opened the front door to this new place that I would attempt to call home, I promised myself once more that this Christian thing was out of the window. My parents had hurt me so much that I could see no link between this and any supposed God who loved the world.

At the same time, I wasn't prepared to declare myself an atheist. I knew there was a God; I was just unsure how He operated – and felt that He wasn't really worth following at all. Here I was, joining the swelling group of young agnostics who couldn't take on a faith and yet were equally unable to totally discard the idea because they desperately wanted to believe in something greater than them.

Why do many young people cling to agnosticism as a form of hope? I'm a great fan of a film called *The Shawshank Redemption*. In this film, the lead character, Andy Dufresne (excellently played by Tim Robbins), is locked up in prison for killing his wife and the guy she was having an affair with, even though he is innocent of both crimes. Once inside and serving his sentence, he receives two weeks in solitary confinement for playing a Mozart record over the loudspeaker system that runs throughout the prison.

On completion of his stint in solitary confinement, he is asked whether it had been worth spending all that time on his own just to have heard that one short piece of Mozart. He says one thing that for me really sums up the situation. He declares that he needs not to forget. Forget what? "That there are things in this world not carved out of grey stone. That there's a small place inside of us they can never lock away, and that place is called hope."[5] The music gave him hope and reminded him of the deeper things in his life that no grey walls could cage.

This same hope is what a lot of adolescents growing up in Christian homes cling to. For them the grey concrete walls can consist of religion, tradition and, if you want a name for it, church. Instead of providing an opportunity for freedom, the church is perceived as trying to take its young people captive. The young person feels trapped, but their hope cannot be taken away. Hope that there's something else; hope that within all the tradition, legalism and hypocrisy that they encounter within the church perhaps there is some truth in the gospel.

Hope that this Jesus guy actually was non-judgemental, loving and the provider of freedom. A simple hope that all the things that the church claimed to be true (and yet are apparently contradicted by their experience of church) were actually somehow possible. A hope that there *is* actually something greater than rituals and committees. The church may try to capture, but the hope cannot be caged. As a result we have many agnostics amongst young people from Christian homes. They aren't totally convinced, but like Andy Dufresne they won't quit hoping that there is something good and true. If hope is allowed to die, then what is left?

Time rolled on in. Danny and I continued getting up to mischief at every available opportunity. In spite of flooding their toilet within three days of moving in

I had found a real home with Rob and Pat, which was well supplemented by Danny's parents when necessary. Rob and Pat and David and Ester (Danny's parents) became vital relationships for me. They supported me when I needed it and played deeply influential roles in my development at this stage. I am, and will always be, very grateful to them for this.

It is fair to say that at this stage life seemed to be going OK. Everything had settled down a great deal since my parents had left and I was starting to get used to my new-found lifestyle. I continued playing football, was doing all right at school, and was still actively exploring the plethora of pleasures that life had to offer. With some satisfaction, I felt sure my parents would not approve. They would live to rue their decision; I was confident of it.

Pleasure for its own sake soon grows boring. It doesn't go anywhere. As time moved on, I knew that I was approaching a point of climax. Something had to give. I was either going to pursue pleasure forever or finally find the truth, if it was out there, for myself. The hope that I alluded to earlier, though hard to pin down, had either to lead to some firm decisions and foundations or be discarded. I couldn't spend the rest of my life speculating about things. There was either truth in the hope, or there wasn't: it really did seem as simple as that. I was to find out either way, and live accordingly.

My eighteenth birthday party drew nearer. This was going to be a great night. I was having a joint party with another friend and it was to be the party to end all parties. My birthday was falling on a

Saturday. Saturdays were brilliant; there was no school to go to, plenty of football to play and an opportunity for a lot of going out. On the afternoon of my birthday I played football for a local team. We won 4–0 and I saved a penalty. This was turning out to be a great birthday. Things would only get better!

Finally the evening arrived. I had set myself a drinking target. Danny and I could handle it. When we'd first started I couldn't really take a lot; two pints and I was away. Yet I'd changed; time had moved on, and now I was a much more expensive date. Tonight I would break all of my personal drinking records. I had reached the landmark of 18 years of age, and my target was firmly set: I would mark this momentous occasion by drinking 18 pints of beer!

The night got off to a great start. More people turned up than I had ever imagined. People from school (some of whom I hadn't invited, as well as the many I had) flocked into the crammed sports and social club in suburban south-east London. The beer was flowing. I was quickly past the milestone of five pints and hadn't even reached for my pocket. Come to think of it, why had I even bothered bringing my wallet?

A couple of dances later I was still loving the night. As someone who usually dances like an elephant, I seemed to be performing brilliantly. The beer kept flowing. By this point I had a line of six pints waiting for my consumption. Being the generous man that I am, I was even giving a couple away. The next hour was committed to reaching my target. Having passed ten pints earlier, I was now progress-

ing past fifteen. Just three more! I was totally inebri-
ated and this just seemed to heighten my enjoyment
of the night. Without beer you could have fun; with it
you could live life the way it should be lived!

It was just after midnight when I finally finished
my seventeenth pint. I really felt rough. My drunken
elation and enthusiasm were concealing quite how
affected I was. One and a half pints earlier Danny had
helped me up after I'd fallen to my knees on the
dance floor. Danny also rescued me after I'd been a
little over-zealous in petting a particular girl. Danny
was, is and always will be, a great friend.

Halfway through my final pint, I went outside
with one of my mates to get some fresh air. I was
explaining to him that I wanted to talk about life
when I was overcome by projectile vomiting. This is
my last clear memory of the night.

What happened after this point changed me forever. Danny and another of my friends helped my
near-comatose body back to his house. I was altogether out of it and actually suffering from alcohol
poisoning. Danny cleared vomit from my mouth and
throughout the night he kept checking that I was OK.
What he did for me was sensational.

I woke up the next morning and proclaimed, "I
don't feel too bad now." At this point I discovered
what Danny had done for me. What Danny had done
caused a monumental change. I left his home and
went to the local park. I had some real food for
thought. If Danny could show me this love, then how
much more could Jesus? In an inexplicable way, the
penny had finally dropped. The love that Danny had

shown pointed me to a far greater love. This Jesus was actually real. He was authentic, even if His people didn't always seem as if they were. The whole thing was so important that I had to make a choice.

That afternoon I fully surrendered my life to Christ on a park bench in Mayow Park, Forest Hill, south-east London. A presence invaded my life at this very moment and the change that took place transformed me forever. I knew it was real: I was no longer alone. I finally understood that Jesus died for Gavin and that He loved me. All this stuff that had previously seemed little more than theory had now become real. When Jesus hung on the cross and felt all of that pain, He was doing it for *me*. This Jesus didn't just want to know other people; He desired to know me. He came to the earth to seek and save all people, and I was no exception. He Himself was the true gift of life, and I was compelled to choose this gift. Therefore I prayed a prayer on that park bench and welcomed Jesus into my life. Nothing would ever be the same again. I would live for Jesus and then once my life was over I would spend eternity with Him in heaven. I was saved!

Two things had played a huge part. First, the example of my parents. They'd shown me that this Jesus thing mattered and that you gave up anything and everything in order to serve Him fully. They loved me dearly, but they lived for Jesus with everything that they had. I never really knew what it meant to love Jesus until my parents left me for Him. This faith that they possessed was totally authentic and spoke volumes to me. My parents' moving to

America initially left me bitter and angry, but the real result was that it pointed me to Jesus. They had been great parents, but I understood what life was truly about only when they showed me what it is that really matters. The greatest thing they ever did was to teach me that the life you live is first and foremost one of personal sacrifice for the sake of the Kingdom of God. As a result, in my moment of need and vulnerability, I found Jesus.

Second, Danny and the commitment he'd shown me. If a person could do that, then how much more would this Jesus do? This question led to a genuine encounter with God that left me in no doubt about the way ahead. Jesus wasn't a truth, a way and a life: He was, is and always will be *the* Way, *the* Truth and *the* Life. I would follow Him for the rest of my days. The commitment I'd shown to football and fun would now be given to the King of kings.

Suddenly I was hit by the reality of my decision. My life would have to change. I would have to speak to people about it. How could I tell my parents after all I'd said to them about their faith? How would the church respond to me now? The whole thing seemed incredibly daunting, though I was sure that I'd made the right decision. I had thought that my battle with faith was the big thing and that this day, if it ever came, would signal the end. Life would be simpler and I would move on swiftly and happily through life. How wrong can you get? This was certainly not the end of the journey. It was only the very beginning.

13 Haven't I Done Enough, Lord?

Many young Christians find the moments following their commitment to Jesus even more taxing than those before. It is far less stressful to be a young person who is unsure about what to believe. Uncertainty can become a habit. It allows the adolescent to criticise everyone else, without commitment. It is a great deal easier to be an antagonist than someone who commits to something. Habitual sceptics can channel all of their energies into critiquing the beliefs of others whilst having nothing to defend for themselves.

Once young people have committed their lives to Jesus, they need to develop fast. Choices have to be made: lifestyle changes, and priorities can no longer remain the same. What seemed like the hardest decision ever (to become a Christian) is followed by a bombardment of new ones, each of which requires an individual response. How do I develop a relationship with Jesus? Why is everyone at church so old? Does it matter that my girlfriend/boyfriend isn't a Christian? The questions, decisions and pressures seem endless.

This is when young people need a great deal of support. The battle for their faith is on. Too often we assume that, because there has been a conversion experience, the hard work is done. The truth is quite the opposite. The pressures, the questioning, the moral dilemmas; it's at this point that the action truly intensifies. Jesus' regular command of "Follow me" is the most challenging one possible. There's no point in doing it by halves, and so young people have a lot to learn. They want to follow Jesus, but other things will still seem attractive. They'll slip up, as I did with drink a couple of times. Yet the key is not which mistakes they make but how they respond to them. They have to explore the realm of faith for themselves and at this time need all the support they can get. The story of Rebecca that I told in Chapter Nine is not an isolated case. Many come to faith and then for whatever reason it all seems too much and they give up almost instantaneously because it is just too hard.

New converts feel very vulnerable. We need to be clear in understanding the strains involved. I remember the period of time immediately after my conversion very well. I really thought I'd sorted myself out and that the future from here on in was clear and simple. The big decision had been made. How wrong I was! My biggest error was that I thought I'd done enough for God. I could see no need for me to do any more, and if anything was quite smug about this. I'd turned my back on rebellion to follow Him; what more could possibly be expected of me?

I felt I was made for university. If someone could have been created for that specific environment then surely that individual was me. I'd looked forward to it for years, had dreamed about it, and was going to have a legendary time. University would be the making of me. I'd always thought about it like this, and had known how fantastic it would be. I would squeeze every last ounce of pleasure from university.

I was sure I would play for the university first XI football team. This would be a great achievement, as the standard was very high, but I was sure that I would be good enough. You never know, I might even make it to captain by the final year! I was a leader, after all. I would spend plenty of time in the student bars and would be sure to find myself wherever all the action was.

Following my somewhat dramatic conversion I was still convinced that this was all more than possible. As a Christian, I would still do all these things that I'd spent many a classroom hour daydreaming about. The only difference was that I'd do them for the King as opposed to for myself. I was convinced that I would be a great witness to the faith in the university environment. I would make Christianity accessible to the masses by being an ordinary bloke with an extraordinary faith. Jesus would be shared through my presence in the student union, the football changing rooms and local public houses.

The difficulty was that God's plans seemed a little different from my own. He wanted me to serve Him, but not in the way I had anticipated. Through what I felt the Lord was telling me and then the outside confirmation of four or five other people, it became clear that instead of university the place for me was actually London Bible College. This was confirmed by a number of people. But *Bible* college: must I, Lord? It seemed like the antithesis of university. Instead of fun there was piety; in place of beer was coffee; instead of a football team a Bible quiz club; and, worst of all, in place of all those fun-loving young heathens I would be stuck with a load of middle-aged Bible bashers. (On arrival, the saddest thing was that these stereotypes weren't as far from reality as one might have hoped.)

There were other possibilities at the time, too. I had been working at my local McDonald's for a couple of years and in my final year at school they offered me a trainee store manager's job on £24,000. This was an awful lot of money for an 18-year-old lad. As LBC became a possibility, the McDonald's idea seemed far more alluring. The other career issue was that I wanted to be a policeman. I would go to university and join the force through their accelerated promotion scheme for graduates. If I were to go to Bible college then I would be giving up on this as well, and effectively training for church ministry.

The Lord wasn't just saying Bible college; He was saying *London Bible College*. Now if Bible college was a bitter pill to swallow, then LBC was bitterer still. As I wrestled intensely with the Lord over this decision, I felt I needed to remind Him of a little of my family history, which had clearly slipped His mind. How had He forgotten that my parents had met at LBC? Their shadow was vast enough, but to enter an environment where they were cult figures seemed ridiculous.

Yet there was more. At the time that my parents had met at LBC, my granddad, Gilbert Kirby, was the principal. Surely I didn't have to enter one of the few places in British evangelicalism where I would be known not only as someone's son, but also as someone else's *grandson*? This seemed ludicrous. Did I have to join the dynasty? Please can I just be myself in the anonymity of university, as opposed to the goldfish bowl of Bible college, where I will be anything other than anonymous amongst a small group of conservative Christians?

After wrestling with God for as long as I could, I knew that something would have to give. I headed off to church one Sunday evening in sheer desperation. The situation had been up in the air for some time by this point. As I sat in the pew I knew that a decision had to be made. I listened for all of the first 30 seconds of the sermon before tuning out. Just as I was ready to go home, the band launched into their final song. As the church belted out the Delirious song "History Maker", I was compelled to fall to my knees. My head in my hands, I had a real encounter with the Lord. I knew at that moment that if I ran away from God's will at 18 years of age then I was setting a detrimental pattern for the rest of my days. Equally, were I to make the right decision at this stage, then I would be setting an edifying pattern for the remainder of my life. The choice was there to be made.

In Matthew 16 Jesus says, "If anyone would come after me, he must deny himself and take up his cross and follow me. For whoever wants to save his life will lose it, but whoever loses his life for me will find it. What good will it be for a man if he gains the whole world, yet forfeits his soul?" (verses 24–26). The message of Jesus is clear, but its practical implications are so very hard to deal with. For the newly converted adolescent, such issues are huge. What do they do? It seems so often that they've already done enough. Yet they have to make further sacrifices.

Jim Elliot was a missionary who went to work with the Auca Indians in Ecuador, South America, in the middle of the twentieth century. The tribespeople he had gone to share the Good News with would spear him to death. In his diary he had written, "He is no fool who gives what he cannot keep to gain what he cannot lose." Elliot learnt in the harshest way possible quite what these words could mean, yet he was completely right. Giving what is temporary is so insignificant when compared to gaining that which is eternal. Bible college (admittedly a far cry from Ecuador) was the last thing I would have chosen, yet it was the best thing for me.

If young people are going to choose not just to follow a faith but also to own one, then very difficult decisions will have to be made. It's not just about an initial decision but also about the choices that come from then on in. Their faith has to move from being "fluffy" to becoming a pragmatic reality. This is such a hard time, but each adolescent needs the love and support of those around as the discipleship process sets in. They've made the commitment, but the ensuing decisions are fundamental to their growth as believers. Do celebrate with the newly converted, but then please love, pray for and support them throughout. They need to begin growing from being baby Christians to those who are mature in the faith.

If their relationship with Jesus develops then everything else falls into place. The rulebook doesn't have to be thrown at the young person straight away. I used to go to a church where a young girl who lived with her boyfriend, took drugs and abused alcohol walked into the building one day and gave her life to God almost instantaneously. The church accepted her and didn't tell her that her lifestyle was wrong and that she couldn't be part of the community until she changed it. Instead the young girl simply got on with it and pursued a relationship with Jesus. She read the Bible, prayed a great deal and just tried to learn for herself.

Two months later she went up to the pastor and said, "Vicar, I don't think drinking like I do is right. Getting off my face seems to be a bad idea. God has told me to stop binge drinking, so I will." The vicar gave her his blessing and encouraged her to keep on going deeper with God. A few weeks later the girl found the pastor again. This time she said, "Vicar, God has told me that drugs are bad; I shouldn't take them, so I'm going to ditch them." The pastor once more gave her his blessing and encouraged her in her faith. A couple more months had passed when she again found the pastor after church one Sunday morning. She said, "Vicar, living with my boyfriend is wrong. We're going travelling in three weeks and are going to get married. God has told me this is the right thing to do."

The beauty of this girl's story is that she found Jesus for herself and then developed a personal relationship. The church was patient enough to allow her

to grow and work out the implications of her decision. As a result, the girl owns her own faith and has
laid down foundations with Christ to last for a lifetime. She has made the right decisions and that's
great. The question is, though, how many churches
are patient enough to wait for young people to draw
their own conclusions? A lot aren't, and as a result
young people either don't develop properly in the
faith, are pushed too soon, or are scared off by the
expectations of others. The rulebook is incredibly
threatening to a new convert, yet given time they can
work these things out for themselves, as this girl did.
When you're in a relationship with Jesus you can
work out the rules and lifestyle implications
involved.

The LBC decision was incredibly difficult. I gave
up one of my biggest dreams in order to follow God.
Had others tried to make me go, then I would almost
certainly have gone to university instead, even
though Bible college was right. I had time to work out
my own faith and begin to live out the truth I had
accepted in my life. Young people need to be supported but mustn't be bullied or manipulated into
decision-making. If they are, then surely they won't
persevere. In fact they may rebel immediately, as they
feel that others are taking charge of them. We've seen
this regularly with our year-out volunteers at Youth
for Christ. Those who have a great year and really
make the best of it are the ones who have made the
decision to do it themselves. The ones who struggle
are those who've been pushed into it by a third party.

The decision to go to London Bible College was

incredibly difficult, but in the end I knew I had to go. It was a choice that would change my destiny forever. Gone was the police and even McDonald's. If I went to LBC then I would enter church ministry afterwards. It was a choice that well and truly set the tone for the future. I decided not to run away from the will of God at 18 but instead to run into it, no matter how difficult. I made this decision because I was given the space to develop, was loved along the way, and was prayed for by a vast array of people.

Please let's do the same for other youngsters. If the decision is theirs, then the pain and difficulties that can follow will be much easier for them to face, deal with and grow through. If the decision is someone else's then who knows what that young person will do when the going gets tough?

14 It's *MY* Faith

My parents had been living in America
for nearly 18 months now, and I had enjoyed being
away from the Christian limelight that I had endured
as a child.

As soon as I arrived at LBC the whole "Christian
celebrity" thing returned, and I found myself back in
the pressure cooker. My first term was particularly
taxing. Everyone wanted to speak about my dad, I
felt, and no one wanted to know *me*. Stories of bump-
ing into Clive Calver in service stations and other
such locations were rife. Even the most trivial of
interactions with my dad were recounted to me with
such enthusiasm that they seemed to have been life-
changing encounters for those telling the tales.

It was as if my dad were some kind of celebrity.
Everyone knew who he was. If my father or brother or
someone had been a huge mass-media celebrity, such
as David Beckham, then fair play, let's get excited, but
a middle-aged preacher man didn't seem quite as
thrilling. He wasn't a big shot; he was Dad. Yet in the
microcosm of British evangelicalism I suppose he
stood out. What a strange world the church is.

Something else that I had to learn very quickly was

that not everyone was that keen on my dad. Most were, but, for whatever reason, some had a real problem with him. It still surprises me today that some people seem to revel in pointing out to me where they feel my dad is wrong. This seems to give them quite a thrill. What seems stranger still is that such people often get quite surprised when I defend him. It's as if they feel it's fair to have an unsubstantiated dig at my father to my face, and then expect me to just stay quiet about it.

At a time when what I really needed was a bit of encouragement, I was actually receiving quite the opposite. One guy who was only a few years older than me took me down to the pub for a drink after our second week at LBC. He thought he was being helpful when he pointed out to me that I was probably saved, but definitely not sanctified. If I wanted to be that then I had to experience Jesus and be washed in the blood of the Lamb. This was the last piece of advice that I needed. Fair enough, I still had things to work on, but I knew Jesus; I was saved. Just because I was quite loud, a tad worldly and a bit raw, this guy assumed that I wasn't really a Christian. If anything was ever going to turn me off the faith that I was growing in then it was precisely this kind of unintelligent narrow-mindedness.

Fortunately, now that my faith was my own, the opinions of others were not so important. I had a relationship with Jesus. This wasn't inherited religion but radical relationship. People could have a go at me or judge me if they liked. My relationship with Jesus was too important for the opinions of others to put me off.

One lecturer in particular helped me no end in

settling in to LBC and feeling at home, a lady called Lish Eves. Lish was legendary. An older member of the faculty, her humour and care helped to compensate greatly for some of what I was facing. Lish affirmed me for who I was but also saw the need for the Lord to prune me; this was just the approach I required. She was a credit to LBC as well as to the Kingdom, and I owe her a great deal.

Things did eventually get a great deal better. I began to enjoy my time there and made some good friends as well. Relationships are so important to the growth of Christians. They seem to be the single biggest factor in faith development. The right relationships will spur one forward to great things, while the wrong ones will just as swiftly point people the other way. Two other lads and I were past masters at both. Just as we could drive one another forward, so all too easily could we hold one another back. Over time we learnt what it was to push one another closer to the throne of God.

If faith is to be nurtured and developed then relationships are fundamental to everything. The most important are those of the boyfriend/girlfriend type. Hundreds of young Christians are negatively affected by their choice of partner. Avowals of evangelism through snogging sound hollow when one considers how many relationships between a believer and a non-believer lead to the believer's spiritual decline as opposed to the non-believer's growth. How often this seems to be the case. My heart cries out for the friends I've seen lost to the Kingdom through wrong relationships.

It's not just the Christian/non-Christian thing that holds people back. I have come across many people who are simply with the wrong partner, even though that person professes to follow the same God. They just don't complement each other. Sometimes such people are too similar, and clash heavily. Others are simply too different, or have very little in common, and that doesn't work well either. Genesis chapter 2 indicates that a man and his wife should be a "helpmeet" to each other. This suggests that Christians should be joined together only if they lead one another closer to God and are able to serve him more effectively together than they can do separately. This all seems so simple, but I've encountered dozens of Christian marriages where this isn't happening. Instead of encouraging each other on in their walk with God, many couples are actually holding each other back.

This marital union can never simply be about spiritual complementarity. You still have to find the other person attractive! Physically your partner should get your pulse racing, and we mustn't pretend as Christians that this isn't important. Physical attraction is fundamental to any marital union – it's just that it isn't everything. Beauty and romance are great but both may fade over time, and neither one can sustain a marriage by itself, although they are important factors in the overall process.

I urge my fellow young people to see their choice of partner as the second biggest decision they will ever make, second only to the one to follow God. Whom you choose to marry can make life either heaven or hell. I was very fortunate, because in my first year at Bible college I met Anne. Beautiful, quiet, submissive Anne. Well, maybe not. Beautiful, most definitely. Quiet, certainly not. Submissive, not sure. When we were going out we discussed questions of the future and following Jesus together. We had to work out how far we were prepared to go for Him.

Anne turned out to be the epitome of a "help-meet". She is able to stand up to me when many others would shy away; she is intelligent, loving and great. Her commitment to Christ is unwavering. She will go wherever, whenever for the sake of the Kingdom. We discovered this by talking it through and not just by following a romantic dream. That wouldn't have been enough. We had to find out whether or not we could achieve more for the Kingdom together than we could do alone. I was lucky: others are not.

Anne helped me set firm foundations of faith. We had been going out for just over a month when I went off one Wednesday afternoon to play football for LBC. That afternoon I was diving down to save a ball during the game when I felt my left arm spasm drastically as my hand and the ball connected. I had dislocated my shoulder. The resulting diagnosis showed that I had a permanent weakness in both shoulders. The joints were weak and as a result my shoulders would continue to come out. I could do certain exercises and undergo an intensive course of physiotherapy, but neither of these would enable me to play in goal again. There was nothing that could be done. I was absolutely devastated!

My dream and the god of my youth were both lost that afternoon. All those hours spent practising wasted; all that equipment now useless; all that enthusiasm unchannelled. I didn't know what to do. I hadn't got any other hobbies. Football had been all-consuming. It had been the one demi-god that I had been able to hold on to. Binge-drinking and the like had been left behind, but football felt as if it were mine to keep. Now even that had to go. I could still play if it wasn't in goal, but what use was that? I'd been a goalkeeper since the age of seven and didn't know how to play anywhere else.

It was Anne who showed me what it was to channel all of my enthusiasm into Jesus. She pushed me on, lived Jesus before my eyes and helped me to attempt the same. She loved me when I had a sling on for six weeks and was very down about my demise as a goalkeeper. I wasn't being that nice, was a little smelly, and was certainly not ideal boyfriend material at the time. Anne cared for me, helped me and listened intently to my endless monologue about losing football. I'm not saying she was perfect, but she came very close.

As I lost football and gained Anne, the faith thing finally discovered some foundations to last a lifetime. It was MY faith. I was gaining in knowledge at LBC, but more importantly my passion was growing too. All the enthusiasm that was previously being thrown into football was now free to be used elsewhere. Anne showed me how to give this extra bit to God. She pushed me closer to Jesus and in turn I learnt to do the same for her. We developed as people and were

deeply enriched spiritually by each other's presence.
I'd lost football but I'd gained massively in the faith.
A huge demi-god had been removed and now I was
free to get stuck in for God completely. The road
ahead was exciting; it was at long last well and truly
MY faith.

These formative stages are so important. We
need Christians with really solid foundations and
strong desires to make a difference. As a church we
need to affirm the importance of decisions and the
effects that these can have for a lifetime. Choices
seem small when you're young but people can still be
living with the consequences of these early decisions
for the rest of their days. Young people need to know
what will stimulate spiritual growth in them.
Equally, they need to know the things that will have
quite the opposite effect.

The first period away from home is the time in
which many faiths live or die. In the university, the
gap year, Bible college and similar contexts, freedom
of choice is fully available to the young person. All the
previous restrictions of the Christian home have
been removed. No longer is Mum there to tell you to
go to church or conveniently leave a Christian classic
on your bedside table. Grace is no longer immediately said at dinner; family prayers are no longer a
mandatory holiday activity. The house is no longer
littered with cross-stitch renditions of Scripture, and
worship music is not automatically in the CD collection. In short, the world that had previously seemed
so undeniably Christian has become far more of an
open book. As parents and as church we need to

release, pray for and fully support our young people at this time.

Whom a young person meets, where they go at the weekends, the films they watch, the life they choose. Every one of these small decisions plays a part in the journey of faith. A strong Christian can very quickly be led astray by the pleasures of the flesh and the world. Equally, a young person can go from strength to strength as they develop for themselves. The key must be that they make their own choices and draw their own conclusions. They need to own their faith, develop in it, and grow. Inherited faith is a waste of time.

15 The Last Battle

*B*y the autumn of the year 2000 I was starting my final year at London Bible College. I had changed. I had been a bit of a rogue, but now I was a respectable (though a little cheeky) final-year theology student. I had really moved on; I knew what I believed and I did all I could to live this out. In spite of a difficult start, LBC had provided an environment in which I was free to grow and change. It had given a lot to me.

I'd always seemed the least likely one of the four children in my family to go to Bible college, and as I was the first to do such a thing everyone was pretty pleased with the outcome. My oldest sibling, Vicky, studied theology at Durham, and both of my other siblings, Kris and Suzy, were to follow me to LBC, but at the time of my going LBC seemed like the most unlikely of places for such a vacillating, headstrong adolescent. Two weeks before the start of the autumn term (having been going out with Anne for a year and a half) I popped the question to her, and we became engaged to be married in August 2001.

There was still one major thing that the Lord wanted to do. He desired to humble me. I'd fought

145

with Him over what to do next, as I was always desperate not to do as my old man had. Going to LBC in itself was already too much like him. In order to be different I set out a few things that I wouldn't do. Firstly, I promised God I wouldn't preach. Dad's ministry had revolved around his ability to communicate from a pulpit. If I distanced myself from this aspect of ministry then it would be harder for people to make the association between us. This plan failed dramatically, as within four months of joining LBC I'd reluctantly preached my first sermon and by the end of the three years I'd preached in excess of 50.

If I had to preach, there were ways in which I could do this without following my father! Dad had never worked in a local church. I could be a pastor or assistant pastor.

Secondly, I told God that I wouldn't work for any of the organisations my dad had run. This ruled out a large chunk of British evangelicalism (Youth for Christ, the Evangelical Alliance and Spring Harvest) at a stroke.

I felt that these choices were mine to make. I'd weathered the storm of my parents' move, had given my life to Christ, followed Him to LBC and then allowed Him to change me completely. Surely now it was finally *my* turn to choose? Unfortunately it wasn't as simple as that. I couldn't lay down the law with God.

I returned one day from a game of tennis to my room at LBC. There were three new messages on the voice mail. The first was from my mum; the second from Anne. Something struck me immediately about the third message. It wasn't someone that I knew. The voice on this particular message had a strong northern accent.

The northerner was a guy called Jon Burns, who worked for Youth for Christ. He wanted us to meet. I knew straight away that I couldn't; I had no interest at all in YFC. Dad had worked for Youth for Christ, and so it was on my list of places not to seek employment. I felt however that I should mention it to Anne. In her wisdom she suggested that we pray about it. I prayed, knowing full well that I had no desire to hear anything from God, and made my prayer as abrupt as possible. Anne's prayer was a great deal longer, and once she had finished she felt that we had to meet this guy. "Let's at least push the door," she said.

So one Thursday night we headed up to Luton (where Jon lived). My mind was closed. I didn't care what the situation was, or where the opportunities might be; I had no interest.

Jon spoke passionately about a particular job. Much as I was still fervently against working for YFC, he actually made it sound appealing. A good opportunity for someone else, I thought. His infectious enthusiasm as he spoke of developing and working with young people grabbed us yet I continued to fight it. We left having heard a passionate description of a job to lead a year-out programme called e.t.a. (evangelism. training. action.) and set off back to LBC.

I spent the next few days fighting the whole thing. I didn't want to go to YFC, but it seemed so right. But... Dad used to run the joint!

Reluctantly I conceded that I would have to meet

Jon again. Once more he was vivid and passionate in his description of e.t.a. We spoke about the possibility of my sharing the job with Anne and it all seemed to fit together. I spent the next few weeks working seriously through the issues. I wasn't sure that I was ready to humble myself enough and apply for this position at Youth for Christ. But YFC was a chance to fulfil a personal dream that Anne and I both had. It was an opportunity to see Christian young people changed and released into their potential, fulfilling their God-given calling at the same time. What should we do?

Eventually it became more than clear that this was the next step for Anne and me. I had to swallow my pride and work for YFC. This wasn't just pride centred on Dad's previous involvement with the organisation. YFC were based in Birmingham. The last place I wanted to live was up north (though many tell me that Birmingham is actually in the Midlands). I was a London boy. Anything north of Watford seemed a million miles away (quite ironic, seeing that my parents lived in America). The Lord's plans were different from mine. They involved moving away from my beloved London and working somewhere where my dad had once been the boss. In the end I knew what His will was; the hardest thing as ever was choosing to obey.

The tough thing to learn at this stage is that you never stand still in your walk with God. You have to keep going continually deeper with Him. You never arrive until you get to the Pearly Gates; every decision and sacrifice made leads you closer to the next one. Just when I thought I'd arrived, the Lord sent along the next thing needed to humble me. Just to show who's in charge, and that my dreams, hopes and ambitions lie in His hands and not my own. This was the last time when I really battled with God as an adolescent. I called this chapter "The Last Battle" because it was the last battle of my adolescence, yet really there are thousands left to face as one progresses into adulthood.

The end of adolescence is all about destiny. No longer are the decisions small ones. They now have long-term implications. Whom to marry? Where to work? Where to live? These are all key things. Such decisions often have to be made in one's early twenties, and as adolescence is left behind so these last battles need to be won. If a young person gives his or her life to God, follows this up with a few minor decisions for Him and then gives the big ones about the future to God, then he or she will be in pretty good shape. The stage is set for a lifetime, and a very edifying pattern is put in place. Equally, if a young person gives God only the little decisions and keeps the big ones for him- or herself, then his or her faith will be impoverished. How can you move forward with God and yet not place your decisions, future, lifestyle, relationships and destiny in His hands?

Even at this stage it can seem that young people no longer need the support of the church. However, church support is still crucial. This phase can be one of the loneliest times to be a Christian, especially if the young people have left home. Knowing they have the full support of a congregation who love Jesus too is fundamental to seeing them mature out of adolescence and through into the later years, with the many new challenges that these bring.

Humbling myself and submitting to God was incredibly difficult, yet it was the best thing that I could possibly have done. Young people: please give God the biggest decisions in your life. Parents, youth leaders and pastors: please pray that they do. We'll only really change this world if a generation of people rise up who are prepared to give their all to God. Out of the shadows of so much Christian good over two thousand years let's finally see a generation of people emerge who let God make the big decisions.

Let's see a generation truly fulfil their God-given destinies by seeking Him and following even when it really hurts. It hurts me greatly to surrender myself and follow Him. I nearly didn't. But if young people do it then they are finally choosing life. They are in the middle of where all the action is and are being faithful to the God who knitted them together in their mother's womb.

To see the rise of such a generation takes first and foremost the blessing of the hand of God. Supportive churches, loving parents and committed young people must play their parts. If such a generation of young people can be raised up then this planet will be turned inside out, upside down and back to front. Christ will be proclaimed in every corner of the world and there will be many more celebrating for an eternity in heaven. However, if young people keep the big decisions to themselves, parents remain disillusioned and churches continue to do as they've always done, ignoring the warning signs, then the church will simply continue to shrink, sitting on its ever-growing evangelical rear while the world goes to hell!

Final Thought...

I hope that this book has been helpful to you. Adolescence can be an incredibly daunting journey, and is one that seems to be getting harder. The pressures are growing and the temptations are many. Yet there is great hope! I met Jesus in the midst of my rebellion. We need to pray intensively for our young people and their parents as they go through the hardest of times. I firmly believe that the statistics can change and that, by the grace of God, they will. The church needs to rise up and make a difference.

At no point in this book have I aimed to cause trouble for trouble's sake. It is my hope and my dream that the church can become a place in which thousands of young people lift up the name of Jesus every week. I long for them then to put this faith into action in their communities. I have tried to be constructive in all that I've said, and am genuinely sorry if anything has caused offence.

Now the boot will be on the other foot. No longer am I the young person; now I must be something different. This feeling manifests itself on two levels.

Firstly, Youth for Christ has recently given me a fresh opportunity to make a difference to the numbers of young people in the church. I have been put in charge of the Church Resource Department at YFC and this gives me a practical outlet for my dream of seeing churches overflowing with young people. We must get the message of Christ to adolescents. They need to hear the gospel, so we must tell them. I must now be responsible to my Maker for what I do to help young people in and through the local church.

Secondly, God willing, in the next few years I shall go from being rebellious young person to parent as Anne and I start a family of our own. The greatest compliment I can possibly give to my own parents at this stage is to say that I can't think of anything that I would drastically change with my own offspring from the way my parents raised me. Mum and Dad have been wonderful, and couldn't have done a greater job. I will always be grateful to them for all that they've done. They will never fully know the impact that they've had – and still have – on my life. I just pray that Anne and I can be as good parents to any children of ours. May they come to know the Lord as their personal Saviour and live wholeheartedly in the light of this relationship.

My journey has taken some sharp turns. I long to see my peers doing the same and turning to God. Let's get our youngsters' attention, show them Jesus, and welcome them home.

Notes

1. P Brierley, *Reaching & Keeping Teenagers: Report of the Evangelical Alliance Commission on Evangelism* (London: Scripture Union, 1968).
2. P Brierley, *Reaching And Keeping Tweenagers* (London: Christian Research, 2002), p 129.
3. The *Guardian*, Wednesday, 3 September 2003.
4. C Calver, S Chilcraft, *Dancing in the Dark? Seminar Notes* (Uckfield, Sussex: Spring Harvest, 1994), p 44.
5. F Darabont, *The Shawshank Redemption* (New York: Newmarket Press, 1996), p 65.

Afterword

Over the years there are various names that have been used to describe Gavin. Among the more affectionate are "rascal", "football fanatic", and "lovable rogue". But there have also been more hurtful descriptions. Some people have questioned his depth, sincerity, or even if he is truly a Christian.

You may wonder how this can be. But the answer is quite straightforward. Gavin is the kind of guy who naturally challenges the status quo and threatens the accepted wisdom of his day. He spontaneously disturbs the conventional and that can be a very good thing indeed. It's just that not everybody will like it.

Twenty-five years ago, Ruth's father, Gilbert Kirby, wrote in the foreword of Clive's first book that, while people might feel uncomfortable as they read the book, they needed to be open to the reality that fresh new and younger eyes could identify. There is a fantastic potential for the expansion of the church of Jesus, and conforming to our present realities can never be the right way to achieve it.

Faced by the challenge of a secular and postmodern society, a gentle, passive, cautious Christianity will advance little. What is needed again is a generation prepared to go out on a limb with God – to make mistakes – to grapple with the felt needs of an emerging new society. Change will be inevitable, and we can either support it or resist it. The opportunity is there for young men and women who will help to rock our boat – and move us forward. We can only pray that they will rise to the challenge.

In all of this, Gavin brings salutary warning: let us not expect a new generation of Christians and Christian leaders to rise up by osmosis. They will need our love, our support and our encouragement. They do not need us to hinder them, they face enough obstacles anyway!

As parents, we find it very surprising that Gavin should have written this book. After all, it seems like only yesterday that he first arrived in a hurry and was delivered on the floor of the bathroom! Then the little blond-haired boy with a crooked foot turned out to be a goalkeeper heading for a life in football. Banned from Sunday school, here was the guy who resented Christians but was turned around by the Holy Spirit into a man with such a passion for the church. It all shows that the Lord Jesus is at work among us all, and He still loves to do the unexpected!

That has always been our own dream for Britain. That the church would never be permitted to lapse into comfortable lethargy. Instead, it would be provoked into godly action and activity, and could actually be used to transform the life and destiny of nations. It is an opportunity which we must not miss.

If the price-tag means that the apple cart of our

current condition needs to be overturned, then amen for that.

If we need to foster and encourage a new generation of leaders to rise up and take their place alongside established leadership...

If complacency must be replaced by a sense of renewed urgency...

If those we once expelled have truly become those who now embrace Jesus...

If we have to act differently in order to impact the world... *then let us not run away from the challenge.*

Then we are living at the dawn of an exciting new era, and we face a new tomorrow. "Unconventional", "disturbing", and even "radical" may be the kinds of words we could use to describe Gavin and his friends. Our prayer for this son of ours is that he will never lose the passion that renders him uncomfortable – but that God will shape and refine him into all that he, and others, could be.

Then we will no longer tolerate the weak excuse that we have become disappointed with Jesus. We will not give up in disgust, for He (as Gavin shows) does not give up on us. Instead we can look toward a future in which we serve Jesus with all our hearts and integrate a new future with joy and gratitude. For we must avoid living and acting in a way that means Jesus could ever be disappointed with us.

Clive and Ruth Calver
Baltimore, MD
January 2004